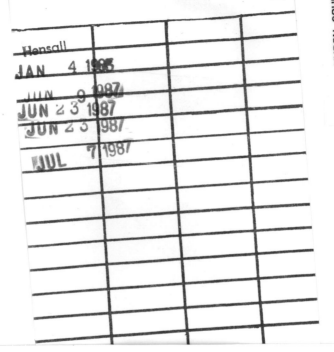

Date Due

Hensall			
JAN 4 1985			
JUN 9 1987			
JUN 23 1987			
JUN 23 1987			
JUL 7 1987			

64114

Mortimer, Hilda.
  You call me chief : impressions of the
life of Chief Dan George / Hilda Mortimer,
with Chief Dan George. Toronto : Doubleday,
Canada, c1981.
  180 p. : ill.

1. George, Dan, 1899-   2. Salish Indians
- Biography. 3. Squawmish Indians -
Biography. 4. Actors - United States -
Biography. I. George, Dan, 1899-
II. Title.
0385048068   1241184 LC

6/Le

You Call Me Chief
IMPRESSIONS OF THE LIFE OF
CHIEF DAN GEORGE

Hilda Mortimer

WITH

Chief Dan George

Doubleday Canada Limited, Toronto, Ontario
Doubleday & Company, Inc., Garden City, New York
1981

"Heaven Haven" by Gerard Manley Hopkins is reprinted
from *Poems of Gerard Manley Hopkins*, 4th edition, 1967,
edited by W. H. Gardner and N. H. MacKenzie,
Oxford University Press for the Society of Jesus.

Library of Congress Cataloging in Publication Data

Mortimer, Hilda.
You Call Me Chief.

1. George, Dan, 1899–
2. Salish Indians—Biography.
3. Squawmish Indians—Biography.
4. Actors—United States—Biography.
I. George, Dan, 1899–
II. Title.
E99.S2G465   970.004'97 [B]

Library of Congress Catalog Card Number: 78-60297
ISBN: 0-385-04806-8
Copyright © 1981 by Hilda Mortimer

For Marion, who shared my journeys

CONTENTS

"And since no way led back,
I voyaged forth over the
dark waters, deeper into the night."

Hermann Hesse
"Flute Dream"

You Call Me Chief

THE MAGICAL, MYSTICAL TIMES

The death canoes were already in preparation for the voyage of the ancestors when the dolphins rode into the inlet that long-ago summer. Racing their jubilant course they came, spinning and diving, soaring in great parabolas, crying and singing to each other in their high, pelagic tongue —cadence heard only in the inner spaces of the sea, as a comet is seen only when it enters the waters of the dark.

It was the first day of the Ninth Moon—the Moon of the Salmon—and for the people of the Western waters, the most important food-gathering time of year.

Running before the dolphins had come the salmon, compelled to their fearful pilgrimage from the vast freedom of the sea to the shallow gorges through which they must climb to their birthplace at the headwaters of the river—to return, to spawn, to die.

The spring snows had been late and heavy, and under the August sun the last glacial rush sped relentlessly down, dashing the teeming fish against the rocks. Already the river's crystal mouth was hazed with blood and silver.

High above his easy prey, the bald eagle spiraled. Black bears, lazing like potentates along the shore, struck with awful swiftness, scooping tired fish to the hollow of cedar roots where the year's new cubs gamboled. Among pale fountains of willow and vine maple tracing the river's course, the blue light of the kingfisher pulsed to and fro.

And the whole upper air was a shrilling of wind-sped gulls.

When the moon rose, white mask-faces of raccoons appeared—nocturnal spirits clearing the day's feast. Before eating, they washed each morsel of food with a kind of delicate reverence, in the phosphorescent August waters. So that, to a nightwatcher, they seemed to be bowing, dipping, turning in their skilled, small hands the luminous talismans of some skeletal feast.

At dawn, and farther out to sea, where the salmon still ran whole and strong, the people of Tsla-a-wat thrust their spears, taking only the fish suitable for smoking, and only enough for the tribe's winter needs. For in the Tsla-a-wat was the wisdom of the salmon. And when a great, valiant one escaped the terrors of the river mouth, their spirits leaped with him as he soared upward, through the tormenting fire of August air, to the sweet resting pools between the freshets.

Snug above the level of raging winter tides lay the village, where the women of the tribe worked in the shelter of cedar smokehouses. Wound about with driftwood smoke, their bodies lilted and swayed in the rhythms of sea-harvest.

Some cut and stripped fish for the smoke racks. Others, unfolding their dancers' arms, stretched and swirled cedarbark rope, on which the fish would be strung and stored.

Between sea and fire moved the youngest braves and maidens, gathering driftwood, loading cedarbark baskets with fish from the incoming canoes. In the pause of the afternoon heat, they would race to the rocks, arching radiant bodies to dive and swim as close as they dared to the dolphins.

It was a summer challenge. And the little children would

run dancing down to the gentle waves curling at the shore, to watch with delicious fear the caprice of their brothers. For if they swam too close, the mystical fish, said to love all creatures, would carry them down the many-colored mountains of the sea to the green voids and valleys where even the salmon could not go.

When twilight fell and small brown bodies curled against the mountain cool, legends became real in the glowing pictures of the fires—spirits of totems and the masks of dancers. Suspended in flame, slow-burning knots of cedar were the hollow eyes of the whistling Woman-of-the-Woods who, if the children were not home by sundown, would spirit them away in her sack of cedarbark. Red flame spurting from an arbutus bole was the blood of her breasts, on which proud warriors were said to feed. All the salts of the sea were imprisoned in the driftwood; and in the alchemy of fire they kindled to creatures of air and sea, familiar, yet wholly unknown. With them, the children traveled on their secret journeys into sleep.

From the edge of the forest, where somber tents of fir sheltered the great canoes, came the young Chief Watsukl, followed by the wolf that walked with him always. The time had come to reveal to his people why he had counseled them to make ready the ceremonial canoes, never used at harvest time. Some were already questioning his wisdom, for the Tsla-a-wat knew that if they ignored the gifts that nature offered in her chosen time, there would be none to carry to the neighboring tribes for winter feasting, and hunger would hunt with the cold. The fish would not linger, nor the berries stay their ripening. Each day the bears moved closer to the village, stripping dark wine from salal and wild grape.

But the canoes lay waiting. And Watsukl turned con-
soling eyes to his people and told them that, at the end of
harvest, they must leave this place that had been their
home since the mystical times. They must go to the south-
west, far from the river's mouth. So the White Chiefs had
ordered. And since there was no choice, Watsukl had asked
only that the tribe be permitted to carry the sacred bones
of their ancestors to the new home. The removal of the
dead could not wait for the end of harvest and the on-
slaught of autumn storms. It must begin at the next dawn.
During the coming night, each member of the tribe would
prepare his spirit for the final leaving, and when morning
came, the most noble canoes, guided by the bravest paddlers, would carry the ancestors to a new resting place.

So, in the misty calm of summer dawn, the burial boxes
were borne to the sea. Some were taken from the ground
behind the village; others from trees of the surrounding
forest, where they had hung, from the time of ancient custom, suspended between earth and sky. Many were marvelously carved with aristocratic symbols of power and family
honor; in these lay the dust of warriors and hunters—of
chiefs and noblewomen.

They rode out on the morning tide. Raising their paddles of springing, tireless maple, they turned toward the
sea. And in their sad chant was the sigh of waves, the
mourning of winter woods, and the thousand voices of the
wind. Following came the dolphins.

It was a slow journey. Canoes that could fly under eleven
joyous paddles were guided by only four or five, for they
carried the weight of the dead as well as the living.

It was almost sunset when, beyond a wide turn of the
inlet, they came into a space of startling, reflected light,

quite unlike the shadowed mouth of their river home. There was a rich sea scent of tidal flats, telling of abundant food. The dolphins began at once to feast and play in these opulent waters while the tribal dead were carried to their new burial ground on a grassy rise above low cliffs.

The sun had long set when the canoes were launched on the return journey. In the darkness above the inlet spanned the golden road of the sky, where the souls of the dead walk on their way to heaven. The men of the canoes were comforted to see how brightly its fires shone—campfires where celestial travelers might rest and warm themselves.

The moon rose. The paddlers moved swiftly now over the phosphorescent sea, and so harmonious was their motion, they cast a single fluid arc into the vast, pale air. In their silver wake rode the silver dolphins. They reached the river mouth on the high night tide, curving landward to beach the canoes below their now unhallowed ground.

And then it was that the dolphins, who had so faithfully followed the journey of the dead, circled the canoes four times, soared majestically into the air, and vanished.

And from that time on, they were never seen again in the inlet.

As the dolphins had vanished, so vanished the songs and legends, the lilting Indian names. The new home of the Tsla-a-wat was called by the White Chiefs "Burrard Reserve Number Three."

And in this place, in the white man's calendar year of 1899, was born the great-grandson of Tslaholt, who was the son of Watsukl. And he was called Teswano.

Later, the missionaries who came to destroy his culture renounced his Indian name, and christened him Dan George.

ONE

RECOLLECTION

1966. Spring. Blackbirds and warblers piping in the weedy bank . . . behind them the swish and roar of trucks traveling the highway that has been cut between the seashore and the Indian Reserve, diminishing it by forty acres.

Above the road, the old wood frame houses are set at random on Reserve land, Dan George's tiny three-room plywood cottage at the top of the slope. Scattered along the uncultivated paths is the joyous debris of many loved and wanted children—shoes and toys and small lost socks. An old automobile has been left, not as Reserve garbage, but as a place for children to play; come to the right, true end of old cars, it is like an ancient horse filled with pride of years and now carrying smaller burdens around the pasture.

In the long grass in front of Chief Dan's house lies the faded, blue wooden top of an old truck. On it are painted the words DAN GEORGE AND HIS INDIAN ENTERTAINERS, a reminder of the days when Dan and his children traveled the rodeo and country fair circuits throughout British Columbia presenting their old-style ricky-tick dance music, with dignified Dan twirling the double bass.

The Reserve has changed little since those days, and the stretch of shore, even less.

It is ebb tide. The vast mirror of the tidal flats flashes

pewter light back to the sky . . . illuminates the tall mountains. Across the inlet waters, a city of oil tanks climbs the
leafy hills.

We are sitting on the beach, warm in the shelter of a
felled cedar, which for three years now has been waiting to
be carved into Dan's last war canoe. Leaning against it, he
seems part of this cedar, as he seems always in synthesis
with nature . . . with wind and rain, sunshine and food. In
the nobility of his head; in his eyes, which, except in laughter, seem always on some distant vision; in the poise and
stillness of his body there is a quality of ancientness that
has nothing to do with his age, which this year is sixty-
seven. Perhaps because holding within him a thousand
years of history, he has faced the tragedy of losing that history. For Dan George is the son of a generation of terrible
sadness who lost their lands and culture at one blow, and
were herded from their limitless worlds of nature to the
prisons of the Reserves.

He is a short man, not quite five-foot-seven. But in his
great chest and shoulders is enormous strength, the prod-
uct of years of bush-logging and longshoring. His powerful
hands, mutilated in a childhood accident, are aging now
like the roots of the bronze arbutus, gnarled and twisted
around the life-giving rock to which they cling. These
hands, which have killed with bow and arrow, burned on
the ropes of cargo sailing ships, and held a world of children, are always warm and vibrant to the touch, as if they
hold a secret generator, transmitting healing power.

Close by on the beach, one of many beautiful nieces is
gathering clams. At $.25 a bucket, they will help pay for
her trousseau; she is to be married next year. Watching her
Chief Dan remembers, in the voice that holds the warmth

and smoke of driftwood fire. The tone seems immeasurably deep and the measured pauses are at first disconcerting, until you realize they are part of his inspired sense of timing, lending emphasis or meaning that others might express by increased volume.

His speech has two forms—intimate and patriarchal. When speaking of history he falls naturally into the inherited cadence of the Indian storyteller. In personal matters he tends toward the speech of his boyhood, the result of the struggle to learn a new tongue in a Mission school, where his own language was not only unknown but forbidden. This rather endearing pattern of speech transforms Chief Dan, the classic patriarch, into the loving, ordinary man who drops the occasional "g" and moves his tenses around a good deal.

Today, watching his young tribeswoman gathering food in the age-old way, he is the storyteller.

"When the tide was out like this, it was our greatest joy to run and swim. My brother Harry and I would go with our cousins and spend all day traveling along the rocks, way down beyond where your Second Narrows Bridge is now. There was food everywhere, and we never had mealtimes like today. My mother had a big orchard—hundreds of trees of cherries and plums—but they've all withered now.

"Wild berries were so plentiful we could eat all day from them, or get a worm and fish for tommycod. Before we were sent to school, we had a free, happy life, just as our ancestors did.

"Looking out there now, it seems only a little time since my older brother and I were running free. And now we find ourselves the oldest members of our tribe."

"Is there much food left here now?"

"Come and I will show you."

We walk toward the sea, ankle-deep in the smelly ooze of tidal flats which have been designated one of the richest marine ecologies in the world. Under the rocks, pink and violet sea stars and the huge orange sun star with its twenty arms. Delicious sea cucumbers, like spiny dragons with flowers for heads . . . limpets and winkles . . . moon snails and barnacles . . . purple-feathered sea slugs . . . every rocky surface encrusted with life.

All around us the constant spouting and squeaking—as if from a million tiny geysers—of the underlife of worms and mollusks more bizarre and varied in structure than the inhabitants of any science fiction realm.

Near a little freshwater creek that runs down from the Reserve, we stop to look for clams. Their rubbery necks are protruding slightly above the ooze.

"You see the ones with the round eyes—those are the tough horse clams. The small, long-eyed ones are the littleneck clams—the tender ones—and we still get them plentifully if there's no oil spill.

"And here"—he pointed with his toe to a small sandy depression—"here's the old hole of a crab. They dig themselves deep down into the sand at this time of year, to make their nests and mate. And then they travel"—he gave a broad sweep of his hand toward the steely sea—"like a great tribe, all together, out into the deep water."

The tide had begun to turn, and with it came the biting tidal wind. Walking back to the shelter of the log, I asked why, when the order came to move the Tsla-a-wat people from their river home so long ago, the Chief, his great-grandfather, had not protested.

"He did not have your idea of land. Land was not for

profit, but to provide food and shelter. He only asked that we should have the tidal flats for food, from here, out to where the narrows are." He pointed toward the span of the Second Narrows Bridge, which joins Vancouver to the mountainous shores across the inlet.

"There's a stake and a big chain buried out there still, and that's supposed to be our Reserve too. But how could we ever claim it? That bridge and that highway were built on the land of my granduncle's Reserve on the Seymour River, one of the most beautiful of all our Reserves. But they took it, to put industry on it."

I told him I had recently heard that a shopping center and high-rise complex was planned for the tidal flats area, in spite of violent protests from ecologists and others who recognized its precious quality. There was a rumor also that his own Reserve was slated for development.

"What would you do if you had to leave the Reserve?"

"I do not know. We love this place because my grandfather's footsteps walked here. His voice echoed in these woods. The blood of our people is in this soil. It's a home . . . a place for us. If I left this place"—the soft voice broke —"I would not know . . ." The silver head dropped to his hands in the classic gesture of despair. Tears fell in the sand.

Ten years later, when his success had become legendary, I was to ask that same question and receive a very different answer.

TWO

TRIUMPH . . .

The unexpected break in the life of one who was until the early 1960s simply an average urban Indian, at that time driving the school bus, came prosaically enough.

The Canadian Broadcasting Corporation was then producing a network series called "Cariboo Country." Written by Vancouver *Sun* columnist Paul St. Pierre, the series was being filmed in the wild and marvelous Chilcotin Valley, part of British Columbia's vast ranching territory. St. Pierre is not only a fine writer but a superb hunter and outdoorsman whose years of bush observation have equipped him to render a unique scenario of the incomprehensible— to city folk—mores and humor of wilderness people, cowboys, and Indians.

A major character, developed early in the series, was an ancient Indian, Ol' Antoine, played originally by veteran Canadian actor Eric Vale, a white man. When Vale fell seriously ill, Philip Keatley, the producer of the series, found himself with one week to production time and a great shortage of actors of the required sensitivity. Already cast in a small part was Bob George, Chief Dan's oldest son. One version of the story goes that it was Bob who suggested that perhaps a *real* old Indian might be hired for the part.

"Do you know any?" asked Keatley.

"I'll bring one in for you," Bob replied.

Another version has it that Keatley first spotted Dan's remarkable face in the coffee shop at the airport bus stop, and that it was the late Kay Cronin, an admirer of Dan's working at that time with the Catholic Order of the Oblates of Mary Immaculate, who arranged the first fateful meeting. In any case, after much initial apprehension, Dan agreed to try the part, and as a supportive gesture, Keatley cast his two sons, Bob and Leonard.

Bob George, called Saltann in the Salish tongue, is the elder of Dan's two sons—a highly emotional man rich with warmth and laughter. A powerfully built millworker, he is impressively handsome, with strongly defined features particularly suited to film and television, on which he frequently appears in series like "The Beachcombers." Bob lives with his wife and fourteen children in the old house Dan built for his wife Amy when they married almost half a century ago.

Lennie, baby of the family, is over six feet tall with his father's features, yet still rounded by youth. He was then in his early twenties and in the midst of the '60s youth revolution, wearing his long black hair streaked with silver and ornamented by an eagle feather.

He had recently married Susan, an enchanting white girl, in a typical "flower children's" ceremony, shocking some of the tribal elders by abandoning the accepted family rituals of the Catholic Church. He was, in short, a typically confused and very talented young man of his generation, hoping for an acting career.

With the support of his two sons, the patient intelligence of Keatley's direction, and the respectful admiration of the entire cast and crew, Dan made unforgettable the character of Ol' Antoine, and the series became an award-

winner. Not the least of the factors contributing to his success were the brilliant makeup skills of artist Phyllis New-
man, who found Dan, she says, a marvel of patience and
cooperation. (It took four or five hours to transform Chief
Dan into Ol' Antoine.)

Critics began to describe Chief Dan George as "one of
the finest natural actors anywhere." Yet he was only following a deep instinct that had been masked by the imposition
of a new culture. For acting is the natural heritage of the
Pacific Coast Indian, whose traditions of dance and song,
and especially the brilliant masked rituals of the cult of the
Potlatch, express in theater and magic one of the greatest
cultures the world has ever known—one described by
Claude Lévi-Strauss as being "as worthy of preservation as
anything produced by the Aztecs or Egyptians."

Little more than a hundred years ago, the villages of the
Northwest Coast passed their long, dark winters in a
months-long ceremony. Their stage was a natural one; firm
sand and sculptured stone against the somber backdrop of
evergreen forest. Brilliant masks of the Kwakiutl, feathered
robes of the Haida, and stunning hard-edge designs of the
Chilkat furnished a set lighted by winter fire and torch.
From the watery shadows along the shore, sea creatures
watched—the carved prows of visiting war canoes. And
while the rituals of the Coast Salish had not the artistic
sweep of those of the Northern tribes, their songs and
dances, the winter feasting, and the daily creation of beautiful objects were part of life.

Four years before Canada's Confederation, two-thirds of
the people who produced an unmatched art were dead of
white-borne plague. The death of the culture took a little
longer.

Chief Dan was asked, "Did your own parents pass down any legacy of songs or dances from those days?"

"No. Oh, I remember little snatches of songs my grandmother sang for my younger brothers and sisters, for she lived to be a hundred and ten years old . . . just went to sleep one afternoon, about the time of my seventeenth birthday. In her time, she and my grandfather, Tslaholt, were the great tribal singers and dancers of our tribe.

"But then the Church came. And that was the beginning of the end of our way of life.

"The first Mass celebrated on the North Shore took place right down in my grandfather's smokehouse. They told my grandmother, 'You must forget your pagan ways.'

"And from then on, she was forbidden by the Church to sing or dance. From that time no one ever heard her sing another song in public. And that was very hard for her, for it was part of her life as an Indian.

"You see, we had no writing. Ours is an oral tradition. So in most of two generations it was just wiped out."

It is characteristic of the man that he says such things without bitterness, unlike the majority of Indian spokesmen today who are at last speaking out and documenting that history of emotional deprivation, cruel physical punishment, and cultural surgery inflicted in the name of the various versions of God.

But although the legacy was gone, its spirit remained and was fostered by the new circumstances in which Dan found himself. Cultural differences caused some problems at the beginning of Dan's new career, for he was over sixty when the first opportunity came.

"My main difficulty was to combine the memory of the lines with the necessary voice tone. This means much to an

Indian. Your people speak of inflection, but our emphasis is quite different and much more subtle, for the range is limited.

"At first, too, it was very difficult for me to accept direction from another, and especially a younger, man. But I think all our leaders are actors in some degree. We must develop a kind of acting in order to convince and govern as chiefs and councilors. We must also study the psychology of leadership, and this training helped me."

Perhaps the luckiest accident in Dan's career was his meeting in 1967 with Canada's gifted and courageous playwright, George Ryga.

Ryga was then working on *The Ecstasy of Rita Joe*, the too-familiar story of an Indian girl who, like so many hundreds each year, comes to the city only to be raped and murdered by the very people she looks to for friendship.

The most deeply moving scenes in the play are those between Rita Joe and her father, who comes to the city to try to persuade her to return to her village. In Ryga's original concept, the character of the father was not a major one. On a beautiful summer day, in the golden hills above Ryga's Summerland home, he told how his meeting with Dan inspired him to create one of the most deeply moving roles in theater.

"In him I saw the classic symbol of Indian integrity. I felt that I understood his values . . . the sense of community . . . the continuity of life from generation to generation. Because like him, I had a rural background with minimal possibilities for education.

"At the age of eight I was fully aware that there was no way in my village but to follow in the steps of those who had built it—which meant forgetting any dreams I had as a person.

"But I was educated into a civilization that had already arrived. I could come off the farm and go into an industrial plant without any serious cultural wrenching.

"Dan George, watching his children, is torn; because he knows there is a cultural demise as well.

"For me, the inclusion in the play of the character of Rita Joe's father was the inclusion of the man Dan George."

Dan's superb performance in this role at the Vancouver Playhouse in the winter of 1967 established his star quality and led eventually to all that followed. Overflow audiences left the theater each night in stunned or tearful silence, overwhelmed by the impact of the performances and the content upon their laid-bare consciences.

The effect was perhaps best described by the critic of the Montreal *Star* who, when reviewing *Rita Joe* at the opening of the National Arts Centre in Ottawa two years later, wrote:

"There were some slight technical flaws which could have been cleared up with a little more rehearsal time. But to even mention these would be like quarrelling with the seating arrangements at the last supper."

While all this was going on, Paul St. Pierre had published a book, *Breaking Smith's Quarterhorse*, based on one of the "Cariboo Country" episodes in which Dan had starred. The rights were bought by Hollywood; Glenn Ford was to star as Smith (the title role of the movie) and Dan was asked to audition for his original role as Ol' Antoine.

This time, he panicked.

He was quite unprepared for the summons, which came

not by letter but by telephone to the little plywood house on the Reserve.

The domestic scene that day was typical. Marie, Dan's youngest daughter, who lived at home with her three small children, was washing diapers in the old spiral washing machine. The vintage oilstove belted its heat into the tiny living room where Dan watched television holding his youngest grandson, then an irresistible black-haired duckling. Amy sat at the Arborite dining table, rolling her endless cigarettes. She was a small woman, very still and quiet, radiating a welcoming warmth. And she was strong. Her judgments, when asked for—she rarely gave them otherwise—were clear; and though she never censured, her love and approval were treasured above all else by every member of her family. After forty-nine years of marriage, Dan was totally dependent upon her.

He hung up the old wall phone.

"Gee!" he said, lapsing into boyhood speech. "They want me to go to Hollywood to do a movie with Glenn Ford!"

Amy kept on calmly rolling cigarettes.

"Then you better go."

"I'll make a fool of myself," said Dan. "All them people in Hollywood—they know how to talk and act. They've been to school and college. I don't know nothin' about all that."

"Come," said Amy. "Sit down. And listen to me. You're not goin' to do it for *you*. You're goin' to do it for *us* . . . for all the Indian people. You're goin' to show that we *can* succeed."

Gradually she persuaded him into confidence with the quiet words that have provided motivation for most of

Dan's work . . . the grueling one-night stands . . . the exhausting lecture tours of schools and businessmen's clubs for which he rarely receives any form of compensation. Amy felt as he feels, that each encounter may help the Indian toward wider success and acceptance, toward upgrading the image of the Indian to himself.

Screen tests were arranged for June of that year, 1968, and just before the celebration of their forty-ninth wedding anniversary, Amy and Dan traveled together to Hollywood.

Amy's faith was more than justified.

"HOW AN INDIAN CHIEF CONQUERED HOLLYWOOD," ran the following week's headlines.

For the final screen test Dan was called upon to deliver one of the great tragic utterances of Indian history—the speech of surrender given by Chief Joseph of the Nez Perce tribe of Idaho.

Joseph rebelled in 1877 when the white generals, in contravention of the treaties of 1873, drove the Nez Perce from their ancestral home in the Wallowa Valley. Pursuing their government's determination to exterminate the Indian race, the army hounded, starved, massacred through a thousand miles of wilderness. Joseph and his people were trapped only thirty miles from the Canadian border, where they had hoped to find refuge.[1]

To the last words of Chief Joseph, Dan George brought all the weight of his own history of sorrow and the inner weariness of his people's spirit.

Tell General Howard I know his heart. What he told me before I have in my heart. I am tired of fighting.

Our chiefs are killed. Looking Glass is dead. It is

the young men who say yes or no. He who led the
young men is dead. It is cold and we have no blankets.
The little children are freezing to death. My people,
some of them have run away to the hills and have no
blankets, no food; no-one knows where they are—
perhaps freezing to death. Where is my daughter? I
do not know.

I want to have time to look for my children and see
how many I can find. Maybe I shall find them among
the dead.

Hear me my chiefs. I have fought. But from where
the sun now stands, Joseph will fight no more forever!

Actor Glenn Ford was so deeply affected by Dan's performance that he missed his own cue and spoiled the take.

"Everyone was cryin'," Amy told us later. "Even Mr.
Ford and Keenan Wynn. And the cast were so impressed,
they formed a receivin' line so everyone could shake Dad's
hand. The lady who was on the set to tell the actors how to
speak the Nez Perce language was a real descendant of
Chief Joseph, and she told Dad how he had made her once
again proud of her great-uncle, that she would never forget
him."

Dan made his screen test in one fifteen-minute take and
landed the role.

On another occasion he moved these same colleagues to
tears when, at the cast party after the final shooting of
Smith, he was requested to recite his famous Centennial
soliloquy. This was the first of many soliloquies that would
be created in the ensuing years with the help of Father
Bert Dunlop, a close friend and personal guide. None has

achieved the impact of that first performance in 1967, during Canada's Centennial celebrations.

In Vancouver's Empire Stadium the celebrations took the form of typical Canadian entertainments ranging from square dancing to chuck wagon races. Then suddenly the glaring light dimmed, except for a single spotlight encircling Chief Dan and his family as they moved slowly forward, drumming and chanting. They stopped, Dan stepped forward alone on the vast plateau of the stadium, and when silence came, the tragic questions most Canadians are only now starting to consider rose over a slow, sad chant.

How long have I known you, o Canada? A hundred years? Yes, a hundred years. And many many *seela-num** more. And today, when you celebrate your hundred years, o Canada, I am sad for all the Indian people throughout the land.

For I have known you when your forests were mine; when they gave me my meat and my clothing. I have known you in your streams and rivers, where your fish flashed and danced in the sun, where the waters said: "Come, eat of my abundance."

I have known you in the freedom of your winds. And my spirit, like the winds, once roamed your good lands.

But in the long hundred years since the white man came, I have seen my freedom disappear, like the salmon going mysteriously out to sea. The white man's strange customs which I could not understand,

* Ages or eons.

pressed down upon me until I could no longer breathe.

When I fought to protect my land and my home, I was called a savage. When I neither understood nor welcomed this way of life, I was called lazy. When I tried to rule my people, I was stripped of my authority.

My nation was ignored in your history textbooks— they were little more important in the history of Canada than the buffalo that ranged the plains. I was ridiculed in your plays and motion pictures, when I drank your firewater, I got drunk—very, very drunk. And I forgot.

O Canada, how can I celebrate with you this Centenary, this hundred years? Shall I thank you for my reserves that are left to me of my beautiful forests? For the canned fish of my rivers? For the loss of my pride and authority, even among my own people? For the lack of my will to fight back?

No! I must forget what's past and gone.

O, God in Heaven!—give me back the courage of the olden Chiefs. Let me wrestle with my surroundings. Let me again, as in the days of old, dominate my environment. Let me humbly accept this new culture and through it rise up and go on.

O, God! Like the Thunderbird of old I shall rise again out of the sea; I shall grab the instruments of the white man's success—his education, his skills, and with these new tools I shall build my race into the proudest segment of your society. Before I follow the great Chiefs who have gone before us, o Canada, I shall see these things come to pass.

I shall see our young braves and our chiefs sitting in
the houses of law and government, ruling and being
ruled by the knowledge and freedom of our great land.
So shall we shatter the barriers of our isolation. So
shall the next hundred years be the greatest in the
proud history of our tribes and nations.

As the chanting and the drums died away, there was an
enormous moment of silence, then applause, steady and
throbbing as an answering ritual.

Two years after the Centennial event, those words had
the same effect on his small Hollywood audience. Later,
actor Keenan Wynn accused Dan of always making him
cry.

Although delighted by the warmth and admiration of his
colleagues and crew, Dan found Hollywood—as he does all
cities—too big and boring. He was glad to get back to the
hills by the inlet. But Hollywood was to become an increasing part of his life.

The publicity surrounding *Smith* led directly to the offer
of what was to become Dan's most famous role, that of
Old Lodgeskins in *Little Big Man*, the Arthur Penn movie
based on Thomas Berger's novel.

Ironically, the producers had already approached Sir
Laurence Olivier, then Paul Scofield. Richard Boone
turned down an offer of $300,000 for the part.

Then pictures of Dan as Ol' Antoine came to light; he
was offered, and he accepted, $16,000.

The story of *Little Big Man* is that of another Indian
massacre, this time in Oklahoma, when General Custer

and his United States Cavalry rode one snowy morning into a peaceful Indian village, killed all but a few men, women, and children, then for good measure wantonly slaughtered six hundred horses. The film debunks once and for all Custer's former image as a great American hero.

The filming of *Little Big Man* is recorded by many participants as one of the most grueling experiences in feature film history. On the wall of Dan's house is a framed accolade, presented by the production crew for "endurance above and beyond the call of duty."

Not only his treatment of the role of Old Lodgeskins endeared him to his colleagues, but his incredible physical stamina, derived from so many years of bush-logging and longshoring, enabled him to endure without complaint the excruciating cold of the prairie winter of 1969. On the day of the massacre, over a century ago, it had snowed in Oklahoma; but it had not snowed since in the Washita Valley. So Arthur Penn moved his film location to the plains near Calgary, Alberta, where even the Albertans were suffering from "unseasonable cold."

The December temperatures dropped to −21° F. Wind sweeping down the slopes of the Bow River created a wind-chill factor that sent the temperature down to 60 below. Camera gear and equipment froze, and shooting had to be stopped repeatedly for a thawing out. The crew spent every nonworking moment devising ways to keep warm. Like men in wartime, they compared the virtues of wearing battery-heated socks, Saran Wrap, or cardboard interlining in their boots. One crew member who had tried the last local remedy found that the cardboard had frozen to his socks.

Dustin Hoffman, in the starring role, suffered more than

most. For one thing, he had to ride a horse, and bareback most of the time.

"Horses," he remarked, "weren't made for guys with short legs like me. The whole thing seems to be holding on by clamping your legs around the horse's belly, and mine don't reach."

Many of Hoffman's scenes called for scant clothing, and no amount of technology could bring the heat of an Indian tepee up to Hollywood temperatures. He spent most of the location time blue and shuddering with cold. Referring to Dan enviously one day, he remarked, "Look at him! I'm only thirty-two years old. He's seventy! How does he *stand* it?"

Dan sailed through without a complaint, wearing thermal underwear under his buckskins and, off the set, nothing much heavier than his Cowichan Indian sweater. Afterward: "Gee, it sure was cold," he said.

It was on the *Little Big Man* set that Hoffman asked Dan if he might call him Grandpa. "I never had a grandfather," he told Dan.

"Sure," Dan replied with his slow, warm smile. "I've got so many grandchildren now, one more don't make that much difference."

(There were thirty-seven grandchildren in that year's count.)

And still, when he writes to Dan, or they see each other, Dustin calls him Grandpa.

The release of *Little Big Man* not only brought rave reviews from the critics; it changed forever the Hollywood portrayal of the Indian and brought instant stardom to Chief Dan.

His performance as Old Lodgeskins, the Cheyenne

Chief, has been best described by Judith Crist, the renowned film critic then of the New York *Times*.

Dustin Hoffman's superb performance as *Little Big Man* is matched by that of an honest-to-God Indian (not a Mexican, let alone Anthony Quinn), Chief Dan George.

He epitomizes all that is wise and earthy and noble in old age; his sweetest moment is when, after elaborate death ceremony ritual and incantation (for his own passing) he finds himself still in this world. "Well—sometimes the magic works and sometimes it doesn't," he remarks philosophically. "Let's go home and eat."

His survival is a deviation . . . and a proper one, from the novel. This Indian will not vanish from your memory, and in the film it is the spirit of humanity that endures.

At the age of seventy-one, his silver hair flowing over a purple lamé jump suit, Chief Dan received the prestigious New York Film Critics' Award at the famous Sardi's—restaurant of the stars—in New York. Next day he was nominated for the 1971 Motion Picture Academy Award, the Oscar, as Best Supporting Actor.

He returned home in triumph to find Amy, his beloved wife of fifty-two years, still in St. Paul's Hospital, where she had gone for a brief check on a chronic ulcer condition.

Within a few weeks she was dead.

THREE

. . . AND TRAGEDY

How subtly death announces his coming. The changed rhythms of a body . . . the slowing of a familiar gesture . . . at first barely brush the mind like feathers, then pierce like quills.

Is it resignation, the surrendering of all life's armor, that gentles the rictus smile? Or is the distant look in changed eyes a knowledge of the coming adventure? When do they really leave us?

It was a snowy day in February, glorious, nose-tingling weather that made me choke on the chemical air of the hospital. Over the sigh of the nun's gown, the pneumatic door breathed shut.

Amy turned her head, so slowly, and smiled the soft, radiant smile of a young girl with some new and precious secret.

"She knows," I thought.

At times like these, the "silent language" the Indian understands so well carries all there is of love and concern. There is no need to admonish an Indian patient, "Now don't try to talk!" All is conveyed by the primary communications of eye and touch. Non-Indians have never learned this, in a world where the word "education" means status and survival. If an Indian sees someone approaching, he does not say to you, "Oh look, here comes my friend Charlie. I wonder what he wants." He assumes that since you have eyes, you can see, and Charlie will himself explain his presence if he so wishes. Indians do not indulge in the rapid-fire, half-interrupted conversation that passes, with us, for communication. Their response has well been described as one of "motionless alertness."

The Indian listens with total concentration. Then he silently considers all aspects of his reply before he speaks. It is that pause, the period of "motionless alertness," that has caused so many non-Indians to regard the Indian as "slow." It is simply that he does not waste energy in verbalizing. For this same reason, Dan has often been described by eager reporters as "difficult to draw out in conversation."

George Clutesi, the outstanding painter and author and a member of the Tseshat tribe of Vancouver Island, once told me a story illustrating another aspect of Indian response.

"There was once a meeting at Port Alberni on Vancouver Island. There were mostly white people, but a group of us Indians were gathered in a corner, laughing, joking. One of the white ladies came over and said, 'You seem so happy and relaxed among yourselves. I'd like to ask a question. Why is it that the Indians don't answer when we ask them something?'

"One of our group, a Kwakiutl lady, replied, 'You know, you've always called us stone-faced. You must realize that we think in our own language still, even though it was forbidden to us as children. And when we do answer, we want it to be the best answer we have, because we know that you laugh at us if we don't speak proper English. So therefore, while we're thinking of our reply and how we're going to translate it into English, you answer yourself. So we say—

Chief Dan with his mother and eldest son, Bob, around 1959.

Before...*(Franz Lindner)*

...and after. Dan's transformation to the character of Ol' Antoine in CBC-TV's "Cariboo Country" series, 1964. *(Franz Lindner)*

With ten-year-old Nancy Sandy of the Sugarcane Reservation near Williams Lake, B.C. *The Education of Philistine*, by Paul St. Pierre, won the Canadian Film Award in 1964. *(Franz Lindner)*

With Dustin Hoffman in *Little Big Man*, 1969. *(The Bettmann Archive)*

Special Award presented to survivors of *Little Big Man* shooting. Signed by director Arthur Penn and members of the production staff. *(Tony Westman)*

"Little Big Man"
—Honor Society—
Awarded to
Dan George
For contributions above and beyond the call of duty.
From 112° Above to 44° Below;
From 75 MPH Wind to Rain, Sleet and Snow:
All conditions met and conquered.

1969-70

Receiving acclaim of capacity crowds at *Little Big Man* premiere in
Vancouver, B.C. *(Tony Westman)*

New Year's Day, 1971, with part of the family of twenty-nine grand-children and eleven great-grandchildren. Amy is on Dan's left, Rose is behind her, and Bob is behind Rose. *(Tony Westman)*

Lennie and Susan. *(Tony Westman)*

Amy, four months before her death. *(Tony Westman)*

Amy's funeral in front of the twin-spired church on the Squamish Indian Reserve where Amy was born. Built in 1884, this is the church where Amy and Dan were married and their children were baptized. *(Tony Westman)*

Inside the church. *(Tony Westman)*

that's the answer they want—that's the answer they're going to get!'"

It was George Clutesi who also spoke to me of the white man's interpretation of the Indian custom of touching.

"Your men," he said, "think of this as a peculiar aspect of our people. But we do not touch out of ulterior motives or because we're inclined to homosexuality. We touch because we have trust in our fellow men, and because from the very first light of day our parents have always held us. Every day the parent is expected to put his arms around a child, no matter how big a man that child may feel he is. This grows with us. We get to know a person more deeply, to trust him, through actual contact, instead of talking all the time. It is another aspect of our 'silent language.' The Indian has believed through countless generations that a sick person will be more comforted by touch than by any dose of medicine."

There were few words in Amy George's sick room. She watched the heavy, silent snow.

"Dad phoned from New York," she whispered, "to tell Bob and Lennie to take all the canoes out of the shed. If the shed collapses in this wet snow, they'll all be smashed."

Amy was already hospitalized when Dan left for New York in mid-February to receive the Film Critics' Award.

Lennie had stubbornly protested the journey. At that time Lennie was already twenty-seven years and six-foot-plus of splendid manhood, but he was still, in his mother's eyes, the baby of the family, and his devotion to her was absolute.

"If you go to New York, Pop, that's it for you and me. Don't ever expect to talk to me again. What you're doing doesn't correspond with what I think."

"Okay, son. Thank you for tellin' me what you are feelin'. But what I am doin' would also be your mother's decision."

Next day, of course, it had all blown over as usual.

In the hospital room, the pneumatic door sighed again and two young nieces came quietly in.

"You've come to see my flower garden." Amy turned toward the glowing vases, yet seemed not to see them.

She knows.

Yet only six weeks earlier, when Dan's friend photographer Tony Westman and I had visited the Reserve at New Year's, we had taken the family pictures—all the generations holidaying together by happy chance. I remember that year there were forty-one grandchildren and nine great-grandchildren. We took them hanging out of the trees in the old orchard and later with Amy and Dan, walking on the beach, planning future adventures in the light of Dan's new career.

Before Dan returned from the New York triumph, Amy was sent home to the Reserve. One day I went to visit her at the house of her eldest daughter, Rose. Irene, the third of four daughters, met me with an anxious face.

"I think she's asleep."

In the bedroom, Amy lay quite still, looking through and beyond me.

"What does the doctor say?"

"He says to bring her to the office next Tuesday."

"My God. This is only Wednesday! She's not asleep, she's in a coma. Phone and tell him to come."

An easy thing for a white woman to say, as I was reminded by Irene's downward glance.

"He won't come to the Reserve."

"Then we must get another doctor."

I called my own doctor, who agreed to stand by, though he practiced in a district some distance away. Then Rose called the Reserve social worker. And I was ashamed to see the anxiety and diffidence, the expectation of rebuff, that accompanied that call. But that evening a woman doctor came, and next day the final vigil began in a small hospital closer to the Reserve.

Dan came home from New York, laden with requests for his presence from around the world.

"I'm not goin' anywhere," he said, "till she gets better."

It was early March now. In the clear new air the distant trees were hairs on a vast polar bear's pelt thrown across the mountains. From her bed, Amy could watch the sun rise on these last gleaming mornings of her world. From the lower valleys, where all the perfumes of spring are distilled, balsam and pine, swamp lily, and a thousand others floated up like invisible banners heralding the return of life.

Amy slipped gently in and out, remaining quite lucid for long periods, then succumbing to the ravaging fever. Dan and the many loving relatives came silently to sit with hands resting on her body or gently touching her face. The children brought small exuberant bulletins, but for the most part it was silent communication. On days when Amy rallied to the spring sun, she and Dan spoke of earlier times, reliving their long life together.

Dan recalled how, after living with his parents for the first six months of their marriage, he and Amy bought an old house from another Reserve and tried to fix it up, with no knowledge of carpentry and very little money. They salvaged lumber and old window frames from other Reserve

houses, but, Dan said, "It took me all my time figurin'
out how to put it together. I would just nail somethin' up,
never knowin' if it would fit or not. And I remember
through even the cold winter, we stayed in one room—the
only one that was closed to the elements."

By this time the first girl, Betty, who later died, was
born, and soon Bob, the first son. It would be many years
before Dan built the little plywood shack that is still home.
And then Amy was homesick for the old house, even
though it was no more than a hundred yards away.

She smiled from her bed. "I remember how I cried.
There was too much memories there. I'd raised all my children there. Rose was born there, and my little Glenna that
died in twenty-four hours. And then Ann and Irene and
Marie and Lennie. I can remember saying, 'I don't like it
here. I want to go back home.'"

This feeling of displacement is not a question of distance in the way that white people think of "leaving
home." It is a sense of place, growing out of the Indian's
absolute knowledge of his environment. A tribal location
may have a number of names, all referring to some landscape awareness that non-Indians would never perceive.
These names may refer, not to the whole territory, but to
"the little rise where the maples grow." The little rise may
be so slight as to be almost imperceptible, but it is an important and familiar landmark to the hunter and tracker.
And while urban Indians no longer follow these ways, the
intuitive perception is still there. So that to Amy, the hundred yards between her old house and the new one repre-
sented a great uprooting.

Sometimes Dan would talk of improving the new house.
"She always wanted a big front porch to sit out on in the

good weather. Maybe I'll get around to it this year." This had been a family joke for years; for although Dan had installed the porch door, twelve feet above the ground and nailed shut, he'd never got the porch on. Yet he spoke of it now as though Amy would soon be coming home.

On a snowy evening the call came. I reached the hospital at nine-thirty, well past formal visiting hours. All accommodation for visitors was closed. Across from the elevator door was an alcove, about eight feet wide, in the harsh tiled wall. I think it was blue, though I remember only the ghastly clinical light and the frieze of stricken faces. Dan leaned, half-collapsed, against the wall. No one had thought to bring him a chair. Some kneeled or sat on the floor.

In Amy's room, others had gathered to say good-bye. Lennie bent with his face touching her pillow. I put my snow-cold hands on her fiery temples.

"Who is it?"

I told her.

"They asked me where the ice caves were," she whispered. Then: "Where did Lennie get that knife?"

She had reentered the haze, yet still her great strength held her to life.

Amy George came from that line of women who in older generations were the core and strength of the family—its real guiding power. She was born of strong parents. Her father, Henry Jack, was a powerful and intelligent leader, both among the Squamish people and on the labor front. From all reports, Amy's mother was a dynamo. A friend recalled how he would watch that remarkable lady pack the carcass of a hundred-and-fifty-pound deer on her back, hang it from a rafter, and proceed to skin it, not with a knife, but with her bare hands. She thought nothing of hauling a hundred-pound sack of wheat up the slope from the supply canoes, and is remembered still as a relentless driving force behind her sons and grandsons in the great annual war canoe races. Bob George remembers his grandmother with love and terror.

"I've seen our crew out there in the canoe, with our eyeballs poppin' out, and foamin' at the mouth. We didn't *get* out of the canoe, we *fell* out. But we won. We had to. My grandmother was standin' out on the beach, knee-deep in water, with the tide comin' in on her. They said to her 'Ta-a [that's Grandmother], you're in the water, you'll freeze.' But she stood there all through the race. 'I can stand here if I like. They're my damn feet,' she'd say. 'Those are my sons out there.'"

Although Amy George's nature was more gentle, she had inherited her mother's spirit and power. She was never for a moment in doubt of the worth of her Indian-ness, and against her firm shores beat all the storms and eddies of more uncertain lives.

The prospect of losing her guidance and wisdom was especially painful for the young men of the family, a generation now removed almost entirely from traditional ways of survival, forced into unequal competition in a world where all material and cultural values are stacked against them. In the early years of doubt and confusion, Amy gave total support to their young manhood. Dan had always relied on her for counsel, and even now, so close to the end, she rallied her last strength to support him. She knew that the following day he must face the gala premiere of *Little Big Man*, and toward midnight, she murmured in a barely audible voice, "You have a big, important day tomorrow. Go."

Exhausted, he left.

Next evening, the Vogue Theatre in Vancouver was jammed, the front rows filled with civic dignitaries. Denis Alphonse, Chief of the Cowichan Indian band, gave the opening address, a biting and witty speech that said a great many truths about contemporary Indian affairs. He ended with these words: ". . . and in conclusion, I will now ask that the white men move to the back of the bus." The civic dignitaries bobbed up and down in their preferred seats, uncertain as to whether this was a joke. It wasn't. Slowly they straggled up the long aisle to the back of the theater, while the Indians marched down the other side.

Dan's opening words came only in a faint whisper:

"You have all heard by now that this has been a difficult time for me. I can only thank you for your good wishes, and hope this film will help your understanding of the Indian people."

It must have been particularly strange for politicians, so out of touch with reality, to watch this revolutionary Western film in the presence of large numbers of native people. The frightful massacre scenes were a complete reversal for Indian viewers, inured to seeing themselves portrayed by Hollywood as ruthless killers. The effect was profound. Whites who had been brought up on the pernicious racism of early Westerns were shocked and disbelieving. Indians identifying with the victims were angered and sorrowful. In that gala audience, many faces were covered, in horror and in shame.

By the end of that emotionally charged evening, even Dan's great strength had deserted him. He was taken home in a state of near-collapse.

A few days later, early on the morning of March 27, Amy was gone.

FOUR

FAREWELL TO AMY

The house of Rose, Dan's eldest child, is like a cornucopia, overflowing with children and food and the richness of love. It is small and old, like most of the Reserve houses; a frame house with steps and doorways seriously out of alignment, and not much paint or polish. But a new picture window in the kitchen brings light to the dark rooms. Sitting at the kitchen table with its seemingly endless supply of simple food, you can look out to the log booms lying like islands in the inlet, watch the tugboats and crab fishermen and hear the giant throbbing of deep-sea tankers . . . VOOm voom voom voom . . . VOOm voom voom voom . . . vibrating even the mountains behind us. When chill fog shadows obscure the world, you hear the diapason of warning signals, reverberating through an operatic chorus of soprano tugs, baritone fish boats and ferryboats, the rich bass of cargo ships. The oilstove is snug and warm.

Rose and Leslie Thomas have eight children. When the youngest was approaching school age a few years ago, Rose applied for a foster child, finding unbearable the thought of the house without a small child in it.

"No," said the white welfare agents, "you have far too many children to take on the care of another." I wonder if they ever realized what a crime was committed against some unwanted child. Everywhere in Rose's house, children and kittens and puppies romp and cuddle, playing and teasing without friction, as is the way of Indian children.

It was in this house that the wake for Amy George was held the night before her burial.

The rickety front steps were banked with hundreds of funeral flowers, like a cenotaph. From one enormous bouquet a card flashed up like a screen image.

"With sympathy, from the Vancouver Wax Museum."

The door opens.

Rose's beautiful house is a funeral parlor. Gone is the big cozy couch with its cargo of brown bodies. Rows of metallic chairs fill the room, arranged like pews. At the front, anonymous . . . immobile . . . the nuns sit . . . a row of folded black umbrellas.

> "Hail Mary, full of grace, the
> Lord is with thee . . ."

Her nature all disguised, Amy lies under a brutal floodlight.

> "Blessed art thou among women
> Blessed is the fruit of thy womb . . ."

A lost little yellow thing in a vast sarcophagus of fluted satin, icy white.

> "Holy Mary, Mother of God . . ."

She loved pink, red, warmth.

> "Hail Mary, full of grace . . ."

I heard her say, "I never want to be buried in the earth. I want it to be like it was with my people—high up in the trees, with the wind and the birds." Why not a last bed of leaves, cushions of emerald moss, a worthier winding sheet of cedar from her perfumed forest? Anoint her with fecund seeds, the children's precious shells, mermaid's-hair from the sea.

The droning of the nuns is like a sound track from some strange movie, playing itself out with familiar characters in new roles.

As I listen, the lines of Jesuit poet Gerard Manley Hopkins come to mind, written to a nun taking the veil:

> I have desired to go
> Where springs not fail,
> To fields where flies no sharp and sided hail
> And a few lilies blow.
>
> And I have asked to be
> Where no storms come,
> Where the green swell is in the havens dumb,
> And out of the swing of the sea.

"Holy Mary, Mother of God . . ."

What do they feel, under that celestial umbrella? Or do they feel?

Marie comes on camera, the youngest of the George girls. She looks bloodless, demented, her black hair streaming. She falls quickly into hysteria, the only one allowing outward expression of her grief.

Lennie moves across the screen. No eagle feather. No

buckskins. Easy Rider studded jeans. A protest? With Lennie you never know.

Yesterday he said, "If I were to do what my people would do, I would run screaming through the woods."

Tonight his face is blank, drug-erased of pain. He welcomes the chiefs with pride and control. The tribal procession is constant now. Genuflect—lean to touch, kiss, catch the phantom breath.

Irene, Dan's beautiful third daughter, tells us, "Daddy's sleeping. We all went to confession before Mum came home."

Touch, embrace, then out into the healing air and, at the foot of the flowery, unfamiliar door, the life-giving swell of the sea.

I look over to Dan's house. I think of him—apart from the ritual—by himself. I wonder. He has told me that since Amy's death he communes with her spirit for counsel and comfort.

Dan's friend Tony Westman, who did most of the photographs for this book, attended Amy's funeral the next day. Later, he compared the Christian service with his memories of the Indian ceremony of the memorial Potlatch he had once attended.

All of a sudden the ladies just sat down in the front row and the native drummers pounded on a cedar log in visceral rhythm, chanting, and the ladies would just sit there, two dozen of them in traditional dress—just mourning—for two hours or more. And they were in true mourning, not just a performance. They would let the rhythm go through them, as though they became a part of the whole vast reach of tradition. The doors of time opened up, and the matrix of our contemporary society just fell away under the firelight and the drumming. One began to realize that this was mourning for a special person—reliving this person, communing with his spirit. There was no question. It made me realize the value of these situations where you can relive your feelings, fill yourself with a life. With our funerals I have no sense of that filling. I have a sense of the church service, the people coming and watching and doing verbal and physical things. But that's the irony. In these actions you're not allowing yourself to retreat into the full dimensions of despair.

After Amy's death, it seemed that only recollection could find a way through the darkness of Dan's heart. He had retreated "into the full dimensions of despair." Ann Mortifee, who at the age of nineteen sang the lyrics for Ryga's play *The Ecstasy of Rita Joe*, and who later composed the music for the ballet based on the play, composed a song at the time of Amy's death.

> Old weathered man
> Stands by the grave of his lady,
> Old weathered hands
> Reach out to smooth the sand on the grave.
> An eagle flies across the river
> And a lone wolf cries from the hill.
> Old moccasins move away
> So slowly,

Old buckskin coat, held tight
Against the cold.
An old, weathered man cries out
In the forest,
And a young child skips away.
And the circle begins again,
The circle begins again.

FIVE

THE REEL WORLD

Each time I return to Los Angeles by air, I think okay, this time we'll either land on it or crash on it, but we'll never get through it.

Yet we made it again. Down through the belt of Mammon that binds more tightly each day the City of the Angels. It would have to be some angel who, from whatever height of angelness, could sight through that insidious cloud the wild and mystic meeting of land and sea that is California's coastline.

Come to think of it, perhaps the angels still guard their city, immunized, like mosquitoes. Maybe they'll turn into avenging angels and, pollution-fortified, swoop down beating sooty winds and blowing trumpets into a wind that will push the disastrous cloud . . . where? Over the San Jacinto Mountains into Palm Springs?

Not economically feasible. And in Ferlinghetti's Lost Angeles, you must, above all, be economically feasible.

We sank into the polluted sauna of the city on what was probably a sunny morning in April 1971, and immediately began to pick up our cues for the Academy Award rituals to be staged in the next twenty-four hours. In Dan's little entourage were Marie, in Amy's place; Philip Keatley, then Dan's manager and adviser; and me, along to record impressions of Dan in the reel world.

Cameras and action were laid on at touchdown.

Life magazine had first access, since in that year it was still the most commercially prestigious. Mini-skirted writer, tall loping cameraman, both of precisely limited elegance. The degree of this elegance became a reasonably accurate means of determining the pecking order of this reel world.

Later in the day I was to fall into the same trap myself, in a kind of reverse negative exposure.

Dan had brought with him, carefully wrapped in a plastic cleaning bag, a magnificent Plains Indian headdress of eagle feathers, presented to him by fellow chiefs in Alberta. It is unrelated either to the Coast culture or to the body proportions of the Coast Indian. The Plainsman is frequently well over six feet. Dan is about five feet seven inches. Nevertheless, it's his favorite warbonnet.

Life perched him in this dignified ceremonial regalia on one of those self-operated luggage carts, supposedly motorized but really powered by wayward leprechauns, and off he sped . . . wobble . . . wobble . . . click . . . click . . . out to the airport entrance.

A sleek shark glided from the murk, glinted Continental teeth, and disgorged The Studio Reps, a trio of sleek men varying only in height. Faces closed, sexless. Eyes like argillite before the carver moves it to life. Life carves nothing here.

Smooth as piranhas they slid, between Dan and the gathering autograph seekers.

The shark swallowed him up, belched softly, and swam away.

At the Beverly Hilton Hotel, the rooms were *Ladies' Home Journal* erotica, so recently set up that manufacturer's labels still hung from the furniture. ("Crafted with Care for a Century.") Crystal chandeliers, lascivious divans

of brown velvet, roses, rare liquors, pyramids of tree-fresh
fruit.

The *Life* photographer roamed, setting up his shots for
the following morning. Dan was to be surprised having
breakfast in the emperor-sized bed, his pewter hair carefully strewn over seductive pillows of quilted silk.

ABC-TV called to arrange a national network hookup
from the suite.

Reporters called for interviews.

The studio called to say they had arranged a special treat
after the awards—a nice restful weekend in Las Vegas.

The phone rang and rang.

Dan slept, having been up at five to catch the plane.

Marie, too excited to sleep, came to my room to try on
clothes—everything we had both packed. What to wear to
the Governor's Ball?

All the doors on our floor seemed to be open on a world
collage of language.

A gorgeous body undulated by . . . drifts of flame
chiffon . . . eyes lashed and painted to simulate peacock
feathers . . . a crown of hair curlers and, under the evening
gown at four in the afternoon, alligator cowboy boots.

Is she kinky, I wondered, or just comfortable?

Two kimonoed starlets from the Japanese contingent
butterflied in to borrow hair spray, which neither of us had.

The war paint was being applied well in advance.

Our next cue came from The Studio Reps. Cocktails in
Dan's suite.

We walk into a room full of dress suits—black tie, white
tie, and tails such as I haven't seen since British Columbia's
centennial celebration in 1971 aboard her Royal Majesty's
royal yacht *Britannia*, when everyone from press to palace

turned up in hired Moss Bros. suits. As on this occasion, it had been "suggested" by the image makers that formal dress would be appropriate. I recall that photographer Louis Jacques, famed for his elegance, had been overtly instructed, like everyone else, to wear a tie in the Queen's presence. He wore two ties, both fifty-dollar Italian silk jobs on which he exchanged sartorial notes with Prince Philip. He and Philip patronized the same tailor.

But the one-upmanship here takes a different form— precise, calculated. It appears in just what trickle of sideburn, what restrained duck's tail, to sprout. The suggestion of hip—but not too hip ("we don't cotton to that hippie stuff here in Hollywood"). Hip people don't equate with money, and these boys like money. These boys *are* money. Los Hombres en Papel. After my second martini I think maybe they'll all turn green.

But Dan looks so strange. This funeral suit has killed his panache—his shirt of purple silk—his necklets and the rings he wears on every finger.

Perhaps the difference between the New York Film Critics' Award and what George C. Scott describes as "a meat parade—a public display of contrived suspense" is the difference between the purple lamé jump suit in which Dan appeared at Sardi's in New York and this bleak conformism.

Anyway it's time to go.

At the hotel doors, red carpets have already been laid down for our exit, and later on, the entrance of the stars and their manipulators to the Governor's Ball.

The shark is basking at the curb. Dan has trouble moving through the fans. There seems a compulsion to touch him.

Some peck like birds at his clothing.

One has a pair of scissors and tries to cut a piece of his long hair.

We follow Dan's police-escorted car in a station wagon. Beside me, Marie is having periodic cramps and nervous giggles, and she's sweating under her sexy black silk. We are all sweating. The late afternoon heat is oppressive . . . the air like hot acid on the eyes. The driver is filling the car with cigar smoke . . . all the windows closed against the massive traffic.

As a special privilege, we have been given a colored windshield sticker, "Pavilion Parking."

Pushing us along the palmy boulevards are thousands of other cars with colored windshield stickers, "Pavilion Parking."

We are cans full of lemmings, all labeled.

The thick air is a drug. We've been up for sixteen hours. Pattuck . . . pattuck . . . pattuck . . . go the cars, slower and slower. Pattuck . . . I'm in the little fishing boat of Angus Crocker, the Galiano Indian; it's a fish boat with an old one-lung Easthope engine. Pattuck . . . pattuck . . . Angus inches skillfully through reefs of pudding rock to the sea gulls' island, their nesting place.

New-laid clouds, the nests are . . . molded, rounded at the outer edge to float like downy rafts on a spring tide. Gray mist of breast feathers, laced with sea reeds and summer grass . . . the bright gold petals of the sticky daisy. Eggs painted like the pudding rock . . . purple, green . . . golden lichen. Camouflage so exact, in silver caves of driftwood, you might never know the island's secret but for the defending birds.

Screaming attack, they hover barely above our heads. Glaucous gulls, murres, kittiwakes, diving and circling against the white summer sky.

The oyster catchers could kill with those long, blood-red beaks . . . the gulls rip and tear . . . the stubby weapons of the coots drive into our flesh.

They circle closer, screaming a Hitchcock nightmare.

Then somehow the white summer sky shifts, like a cosmic garage door . . . into flat gray bleachers . . . floodlit . . . blinding.

But the screaming grows louder.

I'm awake now, and I see that these are human birds, perched like sea gulls on a ship's railing. The lucky fans in the bleachers who have managed to get tickets for an outdoor view of their gods . . . their rulers . . . for some, their lives.

"AAAaaahhhhhhhh! Kak . . . kak . . . kak . . . AAaaaahhhhhhh! Duke! Sammy! Goldie! AAaaahhhhh!"

"You can tell which way the wind blows by the action of the birds," said Angus Crocker.

As we follow Dan toward the Pavilion, his face is calm, but with a familiar anxious lift to his eyebrows. I realize how desperately important this accolade is, not for him—his is a different kind of pride—but for the hundreds of his people from the Eastern Seaboard to the North Country who expressed their hopes in letters and telegrams.

He sees it as an enormous step on his pilgrimage to up-
grade the Indian's image of himself, to raise that tragically
limited level of expectation.

"Oh, I hope I don't let them down," he had said.

I lose sight of him as we enter the Pavilion rotunda,
which is elegant. The curved and gilded double staircase is
like an exotic river, bearing beauties and beasts; so crowded
it's impossible not to hear people, even if you want not to,
which I don't.

"Chickie, this is Mr. Sherman, not Mr. Herman."

"It's only one little letter. Is that so important?"

"Mr. Sherman is a very important man."

"But he looks just like Mr. Herman."

"Three hundred eighty-five dollars for contact lenses,
and Sherman looks like Herman?"

"But all I said was . . ."

"You only open your mouth to show your teeth, baby.
Remember?"

I am surrounded by snow-capped teeth.

Here's a guy in a snakeskin suit . . . weed wide enough
to wrap a faery in . . . and here's the girl with the peacock
eyes. I try to see if she's still wearing her cowboy boots, but
it's too crowded.

On an even higher wave of screaming, Warren Beatty
washes in. Candice Bergen is there, clean and taut, her disciplined mind showing in that disciplined body.

But except for a few rare ones, there is a surprising con-
formity of dress. The over thirty-fives are in the style of
Richard Avedon's Daughters of the American Revolution,
with corsages. I haven't seen that many corsages since high
school. There's a lot of mink and not-mink, but they don't

seem to know how to handle it. I have a feeling they'll lift it up when they sit down.

I'm glad I've worn my Italian pantsuit. Very low-key. It looks like hopsacking but it's pure handwoven silk, and I can feel the caress of "la griffe" at the back of my neck.

Appropriate to the occasion, *la griffe*—the claw. Instead of being the mark of the haute couture, it should be the Hollywood emblem. They're all hooked.

I see Dan being hustled through the mob in the center of his cold-eyed guardians.

Easiest to spot in the pecking order are the power men, the men with careful eyes. They move toward no one. They stand with paunches draped across their guts like Orders of Merit.

A hand on my shoulder. It's director Robert Altman.

"What are you doing here?"

I tell him.

He looks magnificent in his frilled embroidered evening shirt, quite different from his appearance on location for *McCabe and Mrs. Miller* where, in Vancouver's North Shore mountains, he took on the color of his surroundings. There he was the complete frontiersman; beard, buckskins, mukluks and mud, and the big gold sombrero with its wild bird feathers. When I went there to interview him for the Montreal *Star*, Altman had been kind enough to let me watch the daily rushes for *Mrs. Miller*. I ask him how the film is going and he says they've finished editing and "I want you to know I took out the Indians."

"All of them?"

"Every damn one."

"Why?"

" 'Cause you didn't like 'em."

In the original version of the film, there were some Indian sequences showing the displacement of a small village. On came this bunch of City Indians, wearing every kind of dress from Southern Plains to North Coast. The costume department had gone wild.

Under these noble robes, they were still suburban Indians, and they moved that way. Some even chewed gum as they slumped out of the bush. But when one tried to mount his horse on the wrong side and a little to the rear, I broke up.

I tell Altman I'm glad he took out the Indians.

And now it's time for us to take our own places in the pecking order. Dan, with Philip Keatley, seated close to the stars. Marie, with a group of visiting firemen, a little farther back, and I backstage with the international press contingent, where an equally lethal but more open contest is taking place.

The battle here is for space, international phone circuits, and interviews with the top stars as they come offstage. There are corridors of typewriters and telephones, hordes of press representatives, from Turkey, Italy, Greece, Spain, all steeped in cynicism for the commercial basis of the Academy Awards.

"A humanitarian award for Sinatra? That fucking barracuda?"

I notice later on, that particular correspondent beats everyone to the celebrity wire.

"Why do you think they shot down *Woodstock* as a feature?"

"Forty-three years, and all they can see is fictional narrative and picture-postcard camera work."

"They don't even know there's a different game out there."

"There isn't, man. It's still called box office."

There's a lot of talk about *Woodstock*, and the genius camera work that broke tradition in its use of 16-millimeter film on the wide screen—the kind of breakthrough achievement supposedly the essence of the Awards. Which are now being brought to us, and seventy million others, on a battery of television screens.

There's a lot of betting in the Press Room.

"Fifty bucks says *Patton* will clean up."

"This is military year."

"Gotta do something to buy more time in Vietnam."

"Why do you think they knocked off *Catch-22*?"

They're right. *Patton* takes seven out of ten nominations, including Best Actor, so acidly refused by George C. Scott. It was thought that his chances of winning would be canceled by his blasts against the Academy, but there's Goldie Hawn, seeming quite surprised when she opens the envelope and chirps, "O Migod, it's George C. Scott!"

Then everybody comes over noble, and Frank McCarthy, *Patton*'s producer, tells us how the Academy has "shown what a great organization it is by honoring so generously . . ."

"Horseshit!" says a leading film critic.

Rex Reed had written earlier, "dumpin' the Oscar is like spittin' on the flag." And shortly the flag was there on camera, embroidered on the succulent bosom of some astute, or genuinely patriotic, star.

I recall the bosom but the name escapes me.

When it's time for Best Supporting Actor, backstage betting is heavily in favor of Dan, with two prestigious awards behind him—the New York Film Critics' and the National Society of Film Critics'. As the cameras switch to Dan, he seems very tense, and when the Award goes to John Mills for his role in *Ryan's Daughter*, Dan slumps a little, then turns and smiles.

An hour later, we are back on the red carpet of the Beverly Hilton, waiting for another set of charades to be played out.

Am I looking through the glass of some antic aviary?

Can they get through?

There are hundreds and hundreds outside the glass, floodlit walls of the hotel. I can't get rid of the bird image . . . the claws . . . the feathers . . . the gilded eyes . . . peering and pecking.

For food?

There are more inside the lobby, ten deep along barriers that edge the red carpet leading to the ballroom.

The parade begins. Belafonte, Goldie Hawn, Jeanne Moreau. They all look so much smaller than one expects; even Burt Lancaster, who shows not a glint of the insanity that still takes me back, after five viewings, to every screening of *The Crimson Pirate*.

And they all look masked.

Some pause for a few token autographs. Most are moved on by the continuing parade. The fans demand signatures on their bodies . . . hands . . . wrists . . . shoulders.

And the pleading is like a litany.

It grows stronger for a man I haven't seen before; tall, wary, and with the sexless look I noticed earlier in others. How imploringly they reach for him—and this time it's the men.

"Aw Hughie? Please Hughie? Let me touch you Hughie
. . . just for a second . . . ?"

Good God! I want to laugh. It's *Playboy*'s Hugh Hefner.

He looks like he's wrapped in Saran. He's a super-
package, not a superman.

He could have at least arrived in his famous circular bed,
drawn by teams of bunnies with sable traces.

Oh well, that's Hollywood for you. No panache.

Yet . . . what *are* they reaching for . . . these men?

Of course! Bunny Power!

How accurately Hefner's money men have gauged their
needs.

That animal image.

Bunnies. Soft, seemingly submissive, and easy to fuck.
No response, no responsibility. One of the great North
American syndromes.

"Aw Hughie, just a touch . . ."

He's only a few feet away. I feel that even if they do get
through the Saran Wrap, their fingers will meet cold,
dead flesh.

Anyone for necrophilia?

The litany is lulled as Dan arrives, for he is an unknown
quantity, and the response is tinged with respect. How
beautiful his buckskin face looks in this plastic place.

Marie is lovely, her thick hair a glistening cape, her eyes
gleaming. She loves to dance. So does Dan.

But he looks too exhausted. What a weight he carries up
that triumphal carpet. The disappointment—the bitter
loneliness. Fifty-two years of sharing with Amy, but now
she is not beside him in this remarkable achievement.

I feel her presence like an invisible weight on his arm.

The only thing that's real here is his pain.

The noise, the floodlight, the crush are suffocating.

Suddenly all those imploring arms become long necks with blind heads attached to one monstrous creature, groping mindlessly toward unreality.

One of them brushes my body, and I've had enough.

The tall security guard takes me through gilded ropes, across the red carpet, into empty corridors.

"It's like that every year. The same ones—twelve years now for me—and it's the same ones every year."

"Then it's really two Disneylands. One for children and one for adults?"

"I guess you could say that. Except they make their own. They'll pick one star, and that star becomes their life. They know everything about that star. All they live for is to trade gossip with other people doing the same thing.

"'D'you know what Duke did today?' they'll say. Like he was their family."

"Maybe he is."

"And their houses! They collect movie magazines. Some of them haven't reamed out for thirty years. I've seen 'em —whole rooms—walls of paper—and they live in a little space inside those paper walls."

"Thank you for bringing me back. Good night."

I begin to close the door.

He says, "Don't let it freak you. Some of us are real."

The door says click.

I say, "Are you?"

Marie slept late next morning.

Dan was back to normal, sartorially, in his purple silk and a Navajo necklace. Waiting for the press invasion, he sat on the brown velvet couch watching television commercials.

He loves television commercials.

Ten o'clock. *Life* magazine, scheduled to finish the story begun on our arrival, did not come.

Nor did they phone to cancel.

Ten-thirty. ABC-TV did not arrive.

They did not phone to cancel.

Nobody came, and at noon I said, "It looks as though you're unemployable."

"An artistic pariah," grinned Philip Keatley. "That's what we've got on our hands."

Dan smiled. "I guess we might as well go home."

Marie appeared.

"How was the Governor's Ball?" I asked her. "Did you have a marvelous time?"

"No."

"What happened?"

"Oh, some people sat at a table with us, but they didn't talk hardly at all, and nobody asked me to dance."

"No one?"

"Only Daddy."

We phoned for air reservations. Two-thirty, they said. I couldn't get a flight until the following day.

Marie took sheaves of roses. Dan and I took fresh limes and gin.

Down below, the faithful shark swam up, but this time the piranhas were missing. There was no red carpet, no police escort.

Only, in the back of my head, the faint snap of pearly teeth.

Early next morning I waited at the air limousine entrance, looking down the Beverly Hills boulevards with their manicured homes and gardens.

A car drew up to the house across the street and a secretary got out carrying a briefcase and leading a guard dog. She made the twenty or so steps to the door, pressed an electronic signal, and closed-circuit television at the entrance flashed her image. The door opened. She signaled her safe arrival to the waiting driver and disappeared.

I recalled the story told by a friend of his visit to this Ray Bradbury world.

"About eleven o'clock one night I went out for a walk and a cop car came up and the guy said, 'What are you doing?'

" 'I'm walking.'

" 'Better get off the streets.'

" 'Is there a law? I need the exercise.'

" 'It's your life, man. If I were you I'd get off the streets.' "

A large satiny man joined me at the bus stop. He looked as though he'd been manufactured to specifications. Skin nicely tanned, and filled just to capacity . . . like a good sausage . . . yet not enough to crease or bulge his superb tropical suit.

A Chicano swept globules of soot, drifts of black snow, between the immaculate beds of ground cover that softened the concrete.

"*Buenas días, Señor.*"

"*Buenas días.*"

"*¿Usted te-va en la Línea Aérea del Pacífica?*"

"*Sí.*"

"*¿A qué hora?*"

"*A la siete.*"

"*Buen viaje.*"

"*Muy gracias, Señor.*"

"Excuse me." It was the satiny man. "I've been coming here for seven years and I've never heard him speak to anyone."

"Maybe he knows his own kind."

"You're no Chicano. What kind are you?"

"Canadian, more or less. What I meant was . . . maybe he knows I don't belong here."

"Baby," he said, "nobody belongs here."

Late that afternoon, we sat in the little frame house on the Reserve, with babies and puppies all over the floor and Dan in his old Naugahyde armchair in front of the television set.

"I'm kind of glad now I didn't win. I don't know if I could've carried all that work."

Somebody stuck a head in the door to say there's a black bear cub roaming out behind the house.

"Tell them to keep all the kids in," said Dan. "If they start playing with the little fellow, its mother might come out of the bush."

And he turned back to the television set.

SIX

THE REAL WORLD

Sitting here now with Dan, I remember a summer day in the years before his fame . . . In the room that serves for both dining and living, I sit with Amy at the old Arborite table, drinking tea as she rolls her endless cigarettes. Marie is processing the Indian Reserve banners, endless strings of diapers, at the wringer washing machine squeezed in between the ancient oilstove and the fridge. Marie's three little boys are playing on the floor.

None of the men are at home, and we're talking about love and marriage. Marie confides that she is beginning to recover from her deep love for the alcoholic poet who fathered her first two boys. As we talk about the tragedy of alcohol and the Indian, "Did Dan ever drink?" I ask Amy.

"Like a fish. And gambled. He was so good at blackjack, they called him 'Lucky Dan' along the waterfront. An' it was so easy for them to get booze. They'd just accidentally drop a case or two when a liquor shipment went through, and the boys would share what didn't get broke.

"Later on when the children were growing and he saw how miserable it made me, he tried to quit. One time I took all the kids and packed them off to California—didn't even tell him I was goin'. But with his luck, he went out to the racetrack, won a pile of money, and came down after me.

Bobby and Lennie both got the same problem. I sure hope they can lick it."

Suddenly there is a crash. A budgie cage, which has been added to the few possessions in the room, has been knocked over. The parish priest, on holiday, has left his birds in Amy's care. Reuben, the youngest child, crawling after his brothers, has just collided with the cage, and down it goes. The air is full of feathers, birdseed, and birdshit, the carpet splotched with water.

No one runs to mop up the mess. No one worries about the carpet or the furniture, or scolds the child. Reuben is picked up, comforted, held for a long time until he is ready to go back to play. Only when he feels quite secure again does anyone bother about the mess. I can't help thinking how different attitudes would be in many white households.

I ask Amy, "Do you ever punish your children?"

"Physically? Never! Only once, when we were leaving on a trip with our group of entertainers, Dad took Bobby, our oldest one, and spanked him for somethin' he'd done. I never asked why. I just said, 'Don't you ever lay hands on one of my children again.' And he never did. Beating was somethin' he learned from the nuns at white school, when he was a very young child."

Now, all these years later, when I speak to Dan of this memory, he tells me, "Yes, I think my own stubbornness developed in school from all those whippings. For it is not among our people to lick a child, or scold harshly. My dad would always take me aside, never in front of others, and explain to me why what I had done was wrong. It is much more effective. A beating tends to make a child stubborn or violent. Our people never, ever took a stick or a strap to a child, never in my family. We teach them by example. We scold with kindness, or perhaps tell a story to teach the child what he has done that is wrong. They are led to the habit of sharing with others, and to obedience. Once you have obedience, the rest will follow.

"Above all, we try to instill in them pride. *Tsma-na a-mun-mun.* Be proud. Remember the teachings of your Tsla-a-wat ancestors."

"How powerful was the Tsla-a-wat tribe?"

"My mother had a little idea of figures, and she thought that originally we were more than a thousand, scattered along the shore from Stanley Park to Indian River. The way the story goes, a sailing ship came to this inlet and sailed as far as it could near the mouth of the river where our tribe lived then. My great-grandfather thought by the white man's movements they were trying to find a way back to the open ocean. They also appeared to be charting everywhere they went, and we later knew that this was in order to put in a claim to the lands and territory.

"But they saw so many Indians on the way, our tribe and many others, they realized it would be difficult to dispute the territory. So the story goes that in order to get rid of the Indians, they distributed blankets among them which contained a kind of black fever. In a few weeks the tribes were wiped out. They had no medicines to fight an unknown disease; they simply turned black and died, until only one family of our people was left.

"When the Chief died, his wife, knowing that she was also doomed, wrapped her little boy in a cedar blanket, took him as far as she could from the death place, and placed him in the bush.

"We are then told that a mother wolf, roaming with her cubs, picked up the little bundle and took it to her lair. She dropped it down when she went to nurse her cubs, and the little boy wiggled out and crawled over to feed with them. From then on he grew up as a wolf.

"As he grew, he learned by instinct to make a bow and arrow, and the wolves had great respect for him, not understanding how he could just let a string go, and kill a deer or bear. So they became great companions in the hunt. When he was sixteen, he followed the urge for a mate of his own kind, traveling up Indian River, over the mountains to the canyon of the Fraser River, where he found a bride among the people there. They came back to the inlet and started to build up our tribe once again. Our people have respected the wolves always, and my great-great-grandfather, Watsukl, always walked with a wolf."

"Do you believe that story, Dan?"

He said, almost sternly: "I love and respect every story that is told to me . . . every legend that is passed on . . . even if it does sound funny. When I read some of the books that come from the old country . . . the Bible and others . . . these are hard to believe. But I respect them because they were given to me."

He grinned. "After all, how is a person going to *believe* that a man called Jonah was swallowed by a whale, taken away, and after three days the whale brought him back to shore? That's the kind of a story I'm tellin', but yours was supposed to be believed because it came from the Bible."

"Have you ever been afraid, Dan?"

"Of dyin', you mean? No, especially not now, with her gone."

"I don't mean death. I mean *anything*."

"No. I think it was my schoolin'. It toughened me out so, especially in the early years. Nothin' could scare me after that."

"You went to Mission school?"

"Yes. I was put in St. Paul's when I was five years old. My Dad in his wisdom knew we needed education, for the white people were startin' to come to North Vancouver. My older brother Harry and I were so attached to each other, he refused to go without me, for it was a boarding school. So I went very young."

"How did you feel when you saw your first nun?"

"Oh, it was terrifying for a little boy of my age . . . so strange from the way my mother and grandmother dressed . . . and the priests in their long black robes. They talked another language, even among themselves, for they were all imported from France, you know. And we did not know one word of English, not even yes or no."

"How did they teach you, when neither knew the language of the other?"

"Some of them knew a little English."

"Were you allowed to see your family in those years?"

"Every two weeks we'd catch the streetcar to the end of the line, then walk seven miles to get home on a Friday night. On Sunday, my Dad would hitch up our little team and buggy and drive us back."

"How lonely you must have been!"

"It was terrible. We were forbidden to speak our own language, even at play. And at night we slept in hard beds in rooms like a hospital; we'd never seen things like pajamas before. As you know, in our culture we communicate much of what we feel simply by touching. And our world is full of humor . . . not so serious and morbid. In school everything was the opposite. I seemed to be punished all the time, especially by one teacher who was very stern with me. I remember one day we'd been playing lacrosse and I got into a fight with a tough East End kid who came from a very poor family. There were a few white kids in the school. We fought until we could not go on. And I remember that teacher looked on; I think she hoped he would give me a good lickin' and take some of the spirit out of me. But we just fought on until we could only stand and look at each other. And for some reason I went to him and put my arm around his shoulder, and we shook hands, and from then on we were the best of friends. I remember all my teeth were loose and I had two black eyes.

"Then this teacher who had been so stern took me up to her office, and seventy years later I can still remember her words. 'Daniel,' she said, 'I believe you have the spirit to be a good man. That is why I punish you and whip you and scold you. It's for your own good, because I think you have it in you to be a leader.'

"From then on I worked harder. But I was almost sixteen, and the federal government did not educate us past that age. I remember I cried when I left, for I felt that if I was to get anywhere in life I needed to study and learn more. But I packed my clothes and walked the miles home.

"The very next day I asked my Dad to give me one of his old bucksaws, and I went to work in the bush, makin' shingle bolts. And I worked like that, sunup to sundown, until I was eighteen. And when I was nineteen I got married."

It was an arranged marriage, the request for Amy's hand being made through Dan's parents during a formal visit.

"A week later," he recalled, "we came to Sunday Mass at the Mission Church on the Squamish Reserve, and afterward we met with our parents, and I knew she had accepted me. But she wanted time to reach her sixteenth birthday. She was only fourteen at the time."

Amy was, like her mother, very strong-willed and "highly strung," to use Dan's phrase. And since he is one of the most stubborn men on the face of the earth, it must have been a battle of wills at first. Perhaps tragedy softened the edge of their conflicts. Their first child, Betty, was born a little over a year after their marriage, but her heart was damaged and she died when she was twelve. Another child died within twenty-four hours of birth.

Dan was on the waterfront by this time, and the wild life there did not help things. His tendency toward drinking and gambling was too easily expressed in that brawling world, where, when liquor was not "salvaged" from the incoming ships, the beer parlors of Skid Road were only a few steps away.

During the first six months of their marriage, Amy and Dan lived with his parents. Then he bought the old house and gradually began to restore it. By the time he had closed two of the ancient rooms to the elements, he and Amy were joined by another family member, the oldest storyteller of the tribe.

"My granduncle Seymour came to live with us soon after we got married. At that time he was livin' on his own Reserve with an old couple who could no longer care for him. Amy loved old people, so my Dad made the journey to

Seymour Creek and brought my granduncle home.* I made a little spot for his bed by the kitchen stove, and Amy and I lived in the front room.

"I remember many evenings, just when we'd put out the light to go to sleep, he'd tell stories . . . just begin to talk. I wish I could have remembered, for his words were so very authentic, but I was so tired from doin' hand work in the bush, twelve, thirteen hours a day, I would fall asleep. I do remember how he told of the people who came in here after Captain Vancouver. When the ships sailed into the inlet, the cannon would fire three times.

" 'Boooomm . . . BOOOMM . . . BOOOOMM . . . ,' he always started off that way; and then he'd tell how my grandfather, Chief Tslaholt, and Chief Capilano, and 'Chief Harry'—that was the government agent—would be paddled out by the braves, to trade our furs and beadwork for guns and clothing.

"He'd describe their ships. 'Great big canoe,' he'd say. 'You couldn't paddle the thing. And their clothes . . . pants like underwear, and their shirts hangin' out like washin' . . . and their shoes, all shiny, that made a noise just like horses when they walked.'

"He lived with us for five years. He was still healthy, but just like an old tree that is startin' to wither. He lived to be a hundred and ten, then just went to sleep, like my grandmother."

"Why do you think so many of your family lived to such a great age?"

"It was our food. We never saw pastry or sugar. We used Indian tea—herbs—no stimulants like tea or coffee.

---

* The "journey" was a distance of about one mile.

Nothin' was ever fried. We steamed or barbecued everythin'. Bread was unheard of on the Coast. The Prairie Indians used grain and corn long before we did. But until the sailin' ships came and traded flour, we had never heard of it.

"My grandmother used to make cakes of pounded berries that needed no sugar. They were dried, and whenever you needed energy for your body, you just broke off a piece. Our fish was smoked and stored, and when you were hungry you'd pull some off the cedarbark string and chew it. We did not eat unless our bodies needed to be fed.

"This place was a paradise for food . . . that's what it was called in our Salish tongue—Paradise. So the other tribes, especially the Haidas from the Queen Charlotte Islands, would try to invade our territory, to take food and slaves.

"They came in huge canoes, war canoes maybe ten fathoms long, six feet wide, and six feet high.[1] We would take our stand against them at the mouth of the inlet, near where the Second Narrows Bridge is now. Even a few years ago, hundreds of arrowheads and clubs were found there . . . the tools of war.

"My granduncle used to say, 'These Haidas got nothin' else to do but raid other people's territory and paint their canoes like women.' But of course they were a very great race of Indians, and all the carvings and paintings on the canoes were very important to them. They were also great whaling people. We never took the whale, for we did not need him. But I did hear a story that was passed on, of how the Haidas would paint a huge eye on the huntin' canoe, below the waterline, so that the canoe could see the whale more clearly. Then they would paint black over that

eye, so that the whale would not know it was there. They
were the master artists of all our races."

One day, as we walked down the path leading to the
stream in my wild garden, where Dan likes to sit under the
great cedars, long since logged from his own Reserve, I felt
that his memories were like the paths of the forest around
us. Some travel a little way and vanish. Some are over-
grown and confused. Others seem mere impressions of
moccasined feet on ancient trails. I asked him if he remembered the tribal longhouse.

"No. My grandfather Tslaholt was still livin' in it when
he died, and I was only one year old then. But my grandmother would tell me about it . . . how it was built according to the size of the family . . . three or four generations
livin' together. In this way, everyone learned consideration
for the other, and to respect each other's rights. Our children shared the thought of the adult world, and they were
surrounded by people who loved them, so they learned to
love and trust all people. Today I see people living in
longhouses hundreds of times bigger than my grandfather's, but the people in one apartment do not even know
the people in the next, and care less about them.

"Our longhouse was eighty feet long, made from huge
cedars. Each family was partitioned off with mats made
from bulrush leaves . . . *kiushin* we called them. They
were perfect for insulation. The house was rectangular in
shape, and lined with cedar shakes that smell so sweet. Everyone cooked at the central fire.

"If it was an extra hard winter, they would lay more rush
mats and furs on the floor and walls. In good weather they

had time to gather driftwood and fallen trees . . . we never cut live timber except to build a house or a canoe. They would make plenty of rush mats on fine days, and there was always plenty, so when the snow started to fly, everything was snug and warm."

"Were you carried in a papoose basket when you were a baby?"

His smile was soft with reminiscence. "Oh yes. It was made of cedar roots, very soft, so the baby could wriggle about easily and push his little muscles against it. Carried like that, we were always next to our mother or some relative. We were never, never left alone."

"Do you remember any of the medicines your family used?"

"It's growing all around you," he replied. He got up from his place by the stream. "We would strip the bark from this [cascara] for stomach medicine, and when we were out of work, we'd spread it out to dry, then paddle across the inlet and sell it for two cents a pound to the drugstores in Vancouver. But it doesn't grow on our land any more. It needs other trees, and ours is all logged off. But all our medicines came from the earth and the sea."

"What would you do for this?" I showed him a small infection on my finger, which had been annoying me for two weeks. "I did it with a cedar splinter."

We walked a little way on the path until he found a plantain leaf. He crushed it gently, wound it around my finger, and tied it with a piece of grass.

Two days later it was healed.

SEVEN

THE MARATHON YEARS

From the time of the Academy Award nominations, Dan's life became a marathon of public appearances, films, speeches, and recordings. The grueling schedule he kept in the years following Amy's death would have defeated men half his age. But he welcomed any opportunity for work or travel, the two things that seemed to alleviate the pain of his loss and keep at bay his constant enemy—alcohol.

His commitments were as varied as the geography in which he moved. He might journey from the filming of Walt Disney's *The Bears and I* in British Columbia's Chilcotin wilderness, to the Gathering of the Tribes in America's southern Navajo country. Within the space of a week, he was called on to star in an Easter "Be-In" (he sang "My Blue Heaven" and "Send Me the Pillow You Dream On"), and to consider the role of King Lear, offered to him by the Vancouver Playhouse. Dan had seen British director Peter Brook's assessment of the role: "*Lear* is a mountain strewn with men who failed to make the summit." Or, as Dan put it: "I would have to take a whole year off to do that part."

During Queen Elizabeth's visit to British Columbia's centennial celebrations in 1971, he was a guest of honor at the state dinner held aboard the royal yacht *Britannia*. That same summer he was made an Honorary Con for Life by the inmates of the B.C. Penitentiary.

In 1972, nearing his seventy-third birthday, he went on a month-long road tour, over thousands of rugged miles of British Columbia territory, singing with a rock group known as Fireweed and sometimes doing two shows a day. Shortly before that tour, he was made an Honorary Doctor of Laws by Simon Fraser University, a concrete monolith on the summit of Burnaby Mountain, where as a young boy, Dan had hunted with his father for "gut" food, staples like meat and berries. Now, his small stature all but obliterated by the academic robes and beefeater hat, he sat opposite the former chairman of British Columbia Hydro, Dr. Gordon Schrum, who, by his dedication to the damming of rivers and consequent wastage of land and obliteration of wildlife, represents the antithesis of all that Dan and his people hold most dear.

Along with these contrasting honors came offers of many diverse roles, and Dan continued to accept everything possible, from television commercials to Bob Hope comedies. His actions did not at all fit the image of the noble patriarch and universal father figure created in *Little Big Man* and *Rita Joe*, and Dan was a frequent target of criticism by press and public for playing "undignified roles."

His family, however, made a joke of it.

"I hear you lost your dignity again in that TV show with Hermione Gingold."

"Oh yeah. She was madly in love with me, and I ran away. When she chased me I jumped in my canoe to get away. Then she jumped in after me, and we sank."

"There goes your image again."

"I liked it," he said firmly. "I had fun."

Of his role with Bob Hope in *Cancel My Reservation,*

he said simply, "It's a good story. It's funny, and I die in the end."

What more could an actor ask?

The only roles Dan would not accept were those which, in his mind, might give a negative impression of the Indian. Otherwise, he followed the dictum of George C. Scott that "the business of an actor is to act," accepting so many offers that he sometimes didn't know what his role would be until he actually reached the location. Once, when he mentioned that he was leaving for Arizona, a grandchild asked: "What are you going to do there, Grampa?"

"I don't know yet. Somethin' about a bridge."

When reminded that the Americans had purchased London Bridge and had it shipped, stone by stone, and reassembled in the desert, he grinned down at the child. "Then I guess that means I'll be standin' on London Bridge in my Indian suit."

It is typical of Dan George, and of his whole generation of Indians, that he rarely replies to criticism or explains his actions. It is sufficient that he has made his decision, and he accepts all consequences. He has a very gentle way of dealing with the distorted concept most people still have of Indians.

"Once I was on the plane, headin' for Ottawa to do *Rita Joe* at the opening of the National Arts Centre. There was this man, walkin' up and down, lookin' at me. He looked and looked. I guess he'd never seen a real live Indian before. He went back and forth for a long time, then he came over and said very slowly, 'You. You been long away from Reservation?'

"I just looked straight ahead and said, 'Yes. Me paddle many moons in my canoe.'"

On another occasion, after one of his frequent talks to elementary schoolchildren on the beauty and pride of the Indian heritage: "I felt somethin' tugging at my sleeve. I looked down, and there was a little fellow, about six or seven.

"'Do you still scalp people?'

"'No,' I says, 'we do not do that any more.'"

It would have been possible for him to lecture on the origin of scalping, a custom many people believe to have been introduced by the white bounty hunters.[1] But having seen his own beloved children grow up as "dirty little Indians," labeled by white historians as treacherous, thieving, scalping savages, he knew how it felt to a child to have one's people condemned, and he would not return that condemnation.

"Someday," he said, "he'll learn the truth for himself."

During those marathon years of early fame, Dan was vulnerable on a second front. His own people, especially the emerging young militants, saw in him a powerful political tool. When he refused to identify with the many growing power groups, they were bitterly vocal in their denunciation of him as an "Uncle Tom Indian" or an "apple," red on the outside and white on the inside. At the same time, when expedient, they quoted frequently from his famous soliloquies.

These were the years in which the North American Indian, refusing any longer to remain invisible, began to change the historic stereotype of smoke signals, tepees, and war whoops, and to demand open identification of Indian problems. They were the years of the occupation by Indians of the Bureau of Indian Affairs building in Washington, D.C., and of the fighting of the Second Battle of Wounded Knee. The first had happened in 1890, when Wounded Knee, South Dakota, was the scene of the U.S. Cavalry's most infamous massacre of the Indians. In the spring of 1973, a dramatic confrontation ("Massacre us or meet our demands!") took place on the historic battle site, between one hundred and fifty armed and militant Indians and three hundred FBI agents, Indian Affairs Bureau Policemen, and federal marshals. Although the eleven-day siege ended in a truce, it sparked off Red Power demonstrations all over the continent.

In Canada, the better organized Eastern tribes and the Métis were staging nationwide demonstrations, sending their militant leaders to stir up the less aggressive West. All across the country, Indians were featured in the headlines:

73 HELD AS RCMP CLEAR INDIAN BLOCKADE

INDIANS DEMONSTRATE ON LAWNS OF B.C. LEGISLATURE

INDIANS THREATEN VIOLENCE AT HUDSON'S BAY

Dan disagreed with the bearing of guns by the Indians at the Wounded Knee confrontation. "Here in Canada, we buried the hatchet long ago. Takin' up guns against other people ain't goin' to solve nothin'."

On the one occasion when Dan himself took up a gun, the dust that clouded his image did not settle for weeks. Apparently no one these days expects an *Indian* to shoot a buffalo. Because when he did, and it died, the press went into mourning. If Dan hadn't skinned it so fast, they'd have given it a state funeral.

It happened this way.

Wood Buffalo National Park, in Canada's Northwest Territories, is protective territory for a herd of approximately twenty-seven thousand buffalo. When this population explodes, hunting parties—usually well-heeled American and Canadian trophy hunters—are professionally organized to reduce the number of animals.

In November 1971, invitations were issued to Chief Dan and two distinguished Alberta Indians to join the first Indian buffalo hunt in one hundred years. (It is now history that during the last century, the vast herds that ranged all of the North American plains, and which provided the Indian with food, clothing, and buffalo-hide tepees, were systematically slaughtered by the forces of "law and order," and by bounty hunters carrying out the declared policy of killing or starving the entire Indian race.)

The idea of the buffalo hunt came from Joe Mercredi of Edmonton, Alberta. Mercredi, a Métis convict turned social worker, took the Indian view that the shooting of this particular buffalo would be not a trophy hunt but a sacrifice made for young Indians growing up without heroes.

He felt that young natives in the Northwest Territories, as in other wilderness areas, are forced to leave their families to attend white schools where their skills and cultural values are systematically downgraded. There is no one of their own race to look up to, for native teachers, who might provide a positive image, are still rare.

Said Mercredi, "By bringing Chief Dan to the schools, our native youth were given a chance to meet an Indian who is acclaimed everywhere, and who provides a model for all other Indians.

"There was no question of 'exploitation,' as the press claimed. Our reasons were the same—to improve the young Indian's image for *himself*, not for the *whites*."

Dan had another quite simple reason. He is a great hunter who, for more than half a century, hunted for his basic food.

"I've hunted deer and bear and birds all my life. But I never got buffalo meat. And I thought, 'Gee! Two thousand pounds! That's a lot of meat. It will keep my children and grandchildren provided for a long time.'

"It was an honor to be invited to hunt with the chiefs, and a new experience for me to go after buffalo.

"When we sighted him, I aimed for just below his shoulder, tryin' to get his heart. But he was goin' so fast, I only got his hip, on a dead run at about two hundred yards. They're so huge, they don't seem to be movin' very fast, but they're really travelin'.

"We trailed him easy for about three miles over the prairie; then he headed for the bushland. If I'd had my moccasins it would've been easier in the bush. He ran for some water, to ease his pain. All animals do that. But the little lake was frozen, so he went round the edge, goin' slower and slower and trailin' blood.

"We caught up with him in an open space, and I expected him to charge, 'cause he was wounded. But he just stood, so I finished him.

"Our guide was an Indian, so he understood I was after the meat, for he looked first at the lungs. Then he said, 'No good. T.B.' And I sat down and everything seemed to drain away from me. I was so disappointed."

Pressed by a critical press to explain his motives, he said, "A lot of people told me I should answer back, but as you know, that is not our way . . . to lower ourselves to that standard. Your people do not realize that no matter how much supermarket food I could buy, it's nothin' compared to fresh wild game. That is our natural food.

"And who but an Indian has a better right to hunt buffalo?"

Not only everything Dan did but everything any Indian did was news during that period. Publishers released a veritable flood of books about, and by, Indians. As one reviewer said, "If it's any consolation, the Indian is the Number One guy in the publishing business today."

There is little doubt that the movie *Little Big Man* was a milestone, not only in film making, but in American history. It was a tremendous influence in upgrading the Indians' image of themselves, thereby lending moral support to their political action. Because of his powerful identification with the film, Dan, it seemed, was expected to identify with the new wave of rebellion. Resentment set in when the young, failing to understand the depth of his early tribal teachings, which set non-interference as an unalterable credo, accused him of indifference, of "going Hollywood."

In 1973, the year of the Wounded Knee incident, the Washington Theatre Club in Washington, D.C., invited Dan to re-create his original role as Rita Joe's father in Ryga's play. Possibly it was a move in box-office politics, though the public relations director of the theatre said, "No. We have been trying for four years to get this play. We heard such glowing reports of the Canadian performances."

With Canadian actress Frances Hyland cast in her original role of Rita Joe, the play was a smash. In addition to sellout audiences, delegations of Indian militants occupied the theater lobby after Dan's performance, attempting to persuade him to act as a political spokesman. But he refused to become involved.

"If I was to do that," he said later, "I'd have to spend my whole time studyin' today's history."

He felt that his performance, and Ryga's wonderful play, had made a statement more powerful than any political utterance. And the press was solidly behind him. The Washington *Post* wrote of "scenes of shattering impact, genuine and true, and passages of a purity and intensity that catch you off guard and keep you there. Chief George's scene with Rita Joe . . . when he recalls a story from her childhood . . . is a perfect and probably indelible moment of theatre."

EIGHT

CHANGES

Throughout the hectic months of his first fame, and in spite of public expectation that he would "go Hollywood" and acquire a mansion, Dan returned, between engagements, to the little plywood house overlooking the waters of the inlet he so loves. Though he gave generously to his family, most of his earnings were invested by his legal adviser, for there was little change in his simple personal needs. He seemed scarcely aware of his new wealth. One day as we sat with the tape recorder, we wandered off the subject and began to talk of family matters. I asked him if he had made a proper will, and when he said no, I suggested that it might save a good deal of trouble if he were to do so.

"I want my money to be given equally to each of my children," he replied. "That's what Mum [Amy] wished. Someday, when my lawyer isn't too busy, I'll get around to puttin' that in a will." Then, after a pause, he noticed that the tape recorder was still running. "Anyway," he said quite seriously, "it doesn't matter, 'cause you've got it on tape now."

Without Amy's presence in the old house, it soon became apparent that the somewhat haphazard life-style of his daughter Marie, and the addition of a fourth child in the three-room space, made less than ideal conditions. Dan ate less, and drank more, brooding in that house of memories.

Finally Rose, his oldest daughter, invited him to stay with her family, and under her firm eye and regular domestic routine he seemed stronger. But he does not like to be restricted, even about his health. Eventually he divided his time between the more permissive households of two younger daughters—Ann, on his own Reserve, and Irene, who lives at Mission, sixty miles from Vancouver, on a beautiful hillside overlooking the Fraser River.

Irene's husband, Joe Aleck, is an administrator at the Oblate Mission School, where Dan was a pupil more than sixty-five years ago, and the house is on Mission property. Perhaps he felt happier with those earlier memories, away from recent sadness and from the disintegrating relationships on his own Reserve.

Amy's loss was having a profound effect on all the family, and especially on Lennie, then in his twenties. Because of his hip life-style, Lennie had alienated many of the traditionalists of the family, who also disapproved of his marriage to a white girl. Fair and gentle Susan, steady as a moonbeam, had been an unfailing strength to the whole family during Amy's ordeal, giving unreserved comfort, food, sometimes going for nights without sleep. The physical toll was great, and when her baby was born three months after Amy's death in March, he was a tiny four pounds three ounces. The following December, still in that tragic year of 1971, Susan found him dead in his crib.

Shortly after, Rose called me early one morning to say, "Lennie shot himself last night."

"He didn't kill himself!"

"No," she replied with a resigned sigh, "he never does."

About midnight, hearing a shot, Rose had looked from her window to see Lennie, streaming with blood, crawling up from the beach toward his home. This was his third attempt at suicide since Amy's death, and it occurred, like the previous attempts, after heavy drinking. Bad marksmanship, luck, or instinctive knowledge of anatomy sent the slug precisely into the soft flesh between his shoulder muscles, a relatively harmless shotgun wound.

Later he said, "What would you do, if you lost your mother and your son in less than one year?"

A further sadness came to Dan when the following year, his beloved brother Harry died, removing Dan's strongest support among conflicting family elements. On any Indian Reserve, as in any confined society, there is a great deal of internecine warfare, often due to jealousy over tribal authority. On Dan's Reserve, since nearly all the tribal members are of one family, they have only each other with whom to disagree.

There exists, for instance, a permanent silence between Dan and his brother John, now chief of the tribe.

Many years ago, when the time came for their father, Chief George Tslaholt, to choose his successor, he felt that Dan and his brother Harry, first in line of succession, were too busy enjoying life to take on the responsibility of chieftainship. George Tslaholt was, according to Bob George, "a real stern old guy" who rejected the mischievous ways of his two elder sons in favor of their younger brother John. But John, then fifteen years old, was not himself ready to take on the burden, and he left to live in the United States. Dan was elected in his place, and carried the duties of chieftainship for twelve years. When television and show-business commitments began to intrude on his time, he left office in 1963, and John, who had returned from the south, was again made chief.

But the title, and the recognition, still stuck to Dan— quite legitimately, since he had by this time been made Honorary Chief of both the Squamish and Shuswap bands.[1] However, it was also assumed by outsiders that he was chief of his own tribe, and resentment split the Reserve into two factions.

Dan's daughter Irene was excluded from residence on the Reserve when she married an Indian of another band. This was for generations a common practice, and while it is not so prevalent today, a vote of the band council can still exclude women who marry "off the Reserve," especially in cases of family feuding or council prejudice. Although Indian men who marry white women still retain their Indian rights, Indian women who marry white men may lose not only residence but their Indian status—a reason why many Indians remain unmarried in Christian terms.

But in spite of family conflicts among the elders, Dan's growing influence has brought benefits to the younger members of the tribe, now identified, not as "dirty little Indians," as their parents had been, but as the grandchildren and great-grandchildren of a folk hero. They no longer suffer as Dan's daughters did, who would hide their shoes and clothing in order to avoid the dreaded, clock-controlled hours in white school, and the taunts accompanying the daily journey.

"The first time I heard white kids yelling, 'Dirty little Indians,'" said one, "I looked around to see who they meant. I didn't know it was me."

Another factor has entered the Reserve picture. As a result of the new spirit of militancy engendered by the continent-wide uprisings of the late '60s and early '70s, many young Indians are no longer so anxious to leave urban Reserves. Rose George has been a supportive influence in this area, partly as a result of her father's position, partly because of the new confidence Indians are beginning to feel.

Normally a diffident, gentle person, Rose has pressed for grants to create on-Reserve opportunities in both education and work programs. The old Community Hall behind Dan's house is now an after-school day-care center, a home-coming place for upward of thirty-five children, many from broken homes.

Rose George is a warm, cuddly lady who wears a slightly puzzled frown, as though wondering if she is really going to be able to manage to feed her great brood. Her presence is a joy, transmitting a kind of purity that is generated by her humor and compassion. It is her great concern that trouble for most Indian children starts when they leave the Reserve and enter the aggressive, achievement-oriented world of whites.

Rose has taken nutrition courses to better nourish her after-school wards, who range from preschoolers to teen-agers. In spite of the mixture of ages, you will not see a fight or an unkind act in this varied lot. Helping and shar-ing seem the way of life. Even little handicapped ones are never ridiculed by their peers, never left behind in play. In-deed, they are especially cherished, since they give the op-portunity for love.

Chief Dan has pointed out that if an Indian parent or teacher wishes a child to do something, he accomplishes this by example, or more frequently, by telling a story. The distinguished Indian leader Wilfred Pelletier gives a basic and graphic example of this.[2]

He tells how, as a young boy, he and his friends had been on a blueberry-picking expedition through hot and dusty country. When they came to camp, it was obvious that their feet needed washing before bedtime, but instead of ordering them to do this, their leader told this story:

> There was once a warrior who had a very beautiful body, of which he was very proud. He used to oil and tend his body every day. One day in the woods, he ran into a group of people he had never seen before, and who were hostile. But in his fine shape, he easily outdistanced them. In fact he fooled about and played with them because he was such a good runner. He played hide and seek through the hills and rocks, and then he met another group, who also chased him. He got away from them, but when he met a third group, he suddenly fell.
>
> He tried to get up, but couldn't. So he spoke to his feet. "What's the matter with you? I'm going to get killed if you don't get moving!"
>
> His feet said: "That's alright. You comb your hair and oil your body and look after your arms and legs, but you never did anything for us. You never washed us or cleaned us or oiled us or nothing."
>
> The warrior promised to take good care of his feet if they would only get up and run, and so they did.

Watching Indian children play on the Reserves, you do not see the kind of competition white children are taught from birth. One child may be a fast runner, a more skillful ballplayer, a better swimmer, but he just *is* that way. He has not become that way through parental urging to "beat" others. And the vicious "kill the umpire" psychology so prevalent in white sport is, to a Reserve child, simply incomprehensible.

In this *being* rather than *having* lies the still unextinguished flame of the most treasured of Indian values.

But in this lack of ego-need—to grab, acquire, conquer—lies also the basis of the culture shock the Reserve child encounters in the white school system, where confusion begins.

Happily, more and more young Indians are retrenching, supporting each other in a return to spiritual values. Programs such as those Rose George and her tribespeople are initiating within the Reserve structure contribute to this support. There is a new optimism that the increasing sense of self in the new generations may bring clarity to the confusion that fills our prisons with gifted native people and keeps their suicide rate at the horrifying level of 30.7 deaths by suicide for every 100,000 population, as compared to the national level of 11.9 deaths for every 100,000 non-Indians.[3]

Many young Indians are beginning to realize the advantages of giving up alcohol, and fortunately Lennie George has joined their number. For any youth of the '60s the retaining of traditional values was difficult enough, under the influence of the "flower children's revolution" and their drug-oriented world, which promised, so briefly, an illusion of peace and love. For Lennie, an Indian, the cultural schizophrenia was acute, for he was drawn to both the visions of the subculture and the emerging militants of his own race. Finally, in 1978, after years of alcohol and drug-related problems, he had the courage to commit himself for treatment. He has since become a member of the Mike Rufus Society, named for a recovered Indian alcoholic who spent the last twelve years of his life working with alcoholics on Vancouver's Skid Road. Now Lennie, with his father's support, is working with the society to raise funds for the establishment of a treatment center for native alcoholics.

Watching the changes in progress, it is certain that whatever comes to the new generations, Rose George and thousands of Canadian Indians like her are determined that there is no way back. They must voyage "forth over the dark waters . . ."

NINE

DAYS ALONG THE SHORE

During the marathon years of one-night stands, I saw little of Dan, for he was rarely free, even for a few hours. However, in the summer of 1974, I joined him for a day's outing when he was invited to the annual celebrations of the International Longshoremen's Union, held at Cultus Lake in the Fraser Valley. He had accepted as guest of honor on condition that he would not be asked to make speeches, but could just enjoy the day and perhaps renew acquaintance with some of his companions of the early days along the Vancouver waterfront.

Starting early on a perfect August morning, we drove slowly, avoiding the freeway and taking the side roads through the ripening grain and the hop fields that perfume the lower valley of the Fraser River at harvest time.

The scented air awakened Dan's memories, and he began to talk about the music group he and his family had started in the early '40s, traveling in the big blue wooden truck with its fading lettering, DAN GEORGE AND HIS INDIAN ENTERTAINERS. It still lies somewhere in the long grass of the Reserve.

"It was hop-picking time, like this. We'd pack up the whole family and camp in these fields, pickin' hops and playin' three or four nights a week for dances in the little town halls. The girls were very young—still in school. Rose and Irene and Marie learned how to dance to our Indian songs, Bobby played the accordion, and I played string bass. I'd do all the old corny tricks, twirlin' the bass around in my fingers to fill in the gaps in the music. One of my nephews played the mandolin, and later on when Lennie, our baby, grew older, he played drums.

"When we got good enough, I'd take the summer months off, and we'd travel hundreds of miles through the Interior of the province. At first we played on the Indian Reserve in Kamloops, and the white people didn't come. They seemed not to want to mix with the Indians. So then we hired the town hall, and the Indians didn't come. So we got some posters made, sayin' WELCOME ONE AND ALL, and gradually people started to mix until we were welcomed— sold out, everywhere we went. It made my wife and me very happy to see white and Indian minglin', other than when they were workin' together.

"Then"—he grinned—"we discovered that we could make what was, for those days, a lot of money. People would pay for requests, or give the girls five dollars to sing a favorite number over again. We were playin' mostly in cattle country, so they wanted Westerns . . . Hank Snow, Hank Williams . . . all the old cowboy stuff . . . Amy was our manager, and I think those were some of our happiest times, travelin' together all summer long."

By this time our journey had brought us to the place of the longshoremen's celebrations, Cultus Lake. This lake is the scene of one of the great annual Northwest war canoe meets. In the Indian tongue, *cultus* means "bad water." Indeed it is an evil lake, where treacherous winds course so swiftly through the mountain passes they can swamp an eleven-man war canoe in seconds.

But this day was calm and fair, and later in the after-

noon, in order to escape for a time the hordes of little fans
who are Dan's greatest joy and at times his greatest bane,
we took a canoe to find some quiet spot for a swim and an
hour's rest.

We paddled our rented fiber glass canoe past the shores
of ancient Indian encampments now wall-to-wall with
summer cottages, water skiers, and stinking powerboats.
Dan, one of the great championship canoe pullers of all
time, dipped the paddle with jeweled hands; his pewter
hair flowed in the summer wind, and over his movie star
regalia, he wore an orange fluorescent life jacket, following
water safety regulations as a good example to the children
watching him. He laughed as he recalled the canoe meet
on his own Reserve the previous year, when, in the life-or-
death competition of the fifty-foot war canoes, thirty-six
men were dumped into the frigid waters of Burrard Inlet,
all of them scorning the use of life jackets and their ham-
pering effect on the paddlers' speed.

We beached the canoe on a solitary stretch of sand.
After my dip, I watched him enjoy a good swim. Powerful,
perfectly coordinated, the burnished satin of his skin was
still that of a man thirty years younger, the muscle tone set
long ago by those days of labor in the bush and along the
shore. As we sunned on the white beach, he spoke of the
early days of waterfront life, fifty-four years ago.

Dan's father-in-law, Henry Jack, was one of the most
able and colorful longshoremen on the Pacific Coast, and
through his influence, Dan was able to join the union in
1920, a year after his marriage.

In those days there were a great many Indian longshoremen loading and unloading the ships that sailed and
steamed into Vancouver's vast harbor. Indians were con-

sidered the most expert lumber handlers, for most of them had been hand-logging or in some way handling lumber most of their lives. They had natural balance and superb reflexes as a result of early training in their natural world. They also had great respect for the power of the huge timbers that were loaded in the days of sail.

"Some of the timbers were ninety feet long—so big that when the ship finally got to England, they didn't know how to handle the cargo, and we had to send men over to unload. Mostly I loaded forty-foot lengths. They could only be loaded one at a time, so a five-masted schooner might take anywhere from three to six months to load.

"When I first started, I got forty cents an hour, and some of those who supervised the stowin' might get sixty cents. When I left in 1947, wages was about a dollar and sixty cents an hour. There was no safety regulations . . . nothin' in the way of first aid. Someone might come along to check the gear once in a while, but they were company men who didn't want repairs or anythin' else to hold up the loadin' time. So generally the gear was barely kept up until there was an accident."

Later in the day, we heard other pioneer longshoremen reminiscing about the conditions of those early union days. Work was spasmodic, and men might have to wait to be hired from seven in the morning until seven at night, often in the freezing rain, only to be turned away without work. Even for those within the union, work could go on for eighteen hours, often without a food break. Added to the grueling pace was the danger from inadequately maintained machinery, and the lack of safety nets below the high ladders leading from the docks to the decks of unloaded ships riding high in the water.

Ed Nahanee, a remarkable old Indian from the Squamish Reserve and one of the most effective men ever to represent the Native Brotherhood in its quest for Indian rights, was one who worked with Dan, and who loaded the last sailing ship out of the port of Vancouver. He recalled a day when Dan, having worked without a break for twenty-four hours, threw himself down on the dock, saying, "That's it! I can't go another minute. I'm all in."

"And Dan was one of the tough ones," said Nahanee. "He was quiet but powerful. We have among us what we call 'our big dumb Indian look.' Dan's got it, and he can really put it on when he's made up his mind. I remember one time there was a fight on board between a huge Norwegian mate and a tough little lascar seaman half his size.

"They were fighting below the level of the docks, and regulations said you could only fight on shore. Well, this big Norwegian—he towered over all of us—put up a ladder and climbed to the top. He was just turning to kick the little guy down the ladder when Dan walked up to him with that look, pointed his finger, and said, 'Don't you kick him!' And it stopped him dead, even though Dan only came up to his chest."

Nahanee's memory of the waterfront strikes, described by journals of the time as the "bloodiest waterfront days in history," dated back to 1919, when returning World War I veterans looking for jobs and the reward of a decent place in civilian life became increasingly militant against closed-shop unions.

"I remember one time the union guys had taken a stand in the union hall, armed with clubs and whatever we could find. There were swarms of soldiers storming the doors, and on the roof of one of the warehouses, three machine guns were trained on us by the RCMP, so close I could practically see down their barrels.

"The incident ended in a standoff, but it had a curious ending for me personally. Some years later we had a superintendent named Taylor.[1]

"In talking to my brother and me one day, he remarked that during the nineteen-nineteen strike, he had manned a machine gun on the docks. I said to him, 'Mr. Taylor, did you look closely down that gun barrel?'

"'Why do you ask?' he said.

"'Because if you had looked really closely, you would have seen that my brother and I were in your gunsights.'"

"But," added Nahanee, "that was typical of Indian agents. The government would take men from the armed forces or the police, men with military mentalities who had just a few years to go to retirement, and farm them out to Indian Affairs."

In 1923 came another series of violent strikes that were to go on for many years along the waterfront. The union held out valiantly against the efforts of paid strike-breakers, businessmen, and vigilantes. After more than six months of clubbings and beatings by company police and mounted police who rode even up the steps of houses where women and children were sheltered, the union was broken altogether.

On the way home, I asked Dan about his experiences during those violent times. He told me that he'd stuck it out for several weeks.

"But eventually I took a withdrawal. I had my family to look after by this time, and I had work to do. A lot of the men had nothin' else to turn to. I couldn't afford to stay on the picket line, and I couldn't stand bein' idle. So I went back to workin' in the bush . . . bought a team of draft horses and logged all on my own, up behind the Reserve.

"In those times there was still virgin timber—cedar, fir, hemlock—some of it a hundred and fifty feet high. I cut cedar poles and fir pilin's, anythin' a company wanted to order.

"It was then I achieved what I feel still was one of my greatest accomplishments. I took out the biggest tree on the Reserve—twelve feet through at the base. I started with six blocks and a thousand feet of cable, cuttin' the timber into twenty-foot lengths. In the end I had to call my cousin for help; we got about ten blocks up and finally got the logs down to the water. But they were so huge, no mill could handle them, so they were towed to Seattle and made into lumber there.

"Things were so confused on the waterfront, with strike after strike and our union broken completely. So I kept on loggin' on my own. During the hungry thirties we had to do anythin' we could. We dug clams and sold them for two cents a pound, or we'd pick cascara bark and sell it to the drug companies for almost nothing.

"In the berry season, we'd go up the mountainside, build a shelter of balsam boughs against a big log, and camp out, pickin' thimbleberries and blackberries. Then we'd pack them down to the canoe and paddle across the inlet to sell them in the East End.

"We had a lot of competition from bears in those days, but somehow they seemed to respect our territorial rights. There'd often be a bear on one side of the log and us on the other—but the berries were so plentiful, and we were so busy harvestin', they never bothered us.

"If we were short of meat, sometimes we'd take a bear that season. I remember how berry-tender the meat was; not like it is later in the autumn, when they feed on fish. We were luckier than a lot of white people in those days, for we knew how to find good food.

"From the time I was a little boy, when my father made me my first bow and arrow and a gaff hook, I knew how to get food."

Dan chuckled, remembering one occasion on which he had begun to seriously doubt his prowess in the hunt. It was a day on which he had decided to take Amy hunting with him, shortly after their marriage. He had not yet realized that his young wife was a woman with a heart so tender that she could not bear to see anything killed. She used to joke that for this reason, and because she was allergic to wool, she wasn't much of a Coast Indian woman.

On this unsuccessful day Dan had decided to show his new wife his skill in hunting ducks. When they reached the flats where the ducks would come, Dan instructed her to hide in the reeds behind him, to crouch down and keep perfectly still. Then he waited with hunter's stealth and patience until the ducks came over. At the precise moment he raised his gun, the ducks disappeared. Dan was surprised and annoyed. They tried another spot, and another, again and again. Every time, the ducks seemed to know just what was going on.

"Lucky for me, *you* didn't know!" Amy laughed, telling him about it years later. Of course, the ducks had an ally. When she saw Dan was about to shoot, Amy would suddenly rise from her hiding place, waving her arms! It was a long time before she got up the nerve to tell him about

that day, and by then, he told me, there was not much he
could do but laugh with her.

And in those early days of strikes and depression, Amy
soon came to appreciate his skill in food hunting, when
work was short and money something rarely seen.

In 1936 Dan managed to get back on the waterfront,
where he worked until 1947.

"Then I got hit with a full swingload of lumber. I never
knew what happened. Somethin' must have gone wrong
with the loading gear, because it came towards me so fast I
had no time to get out. It hit me full force on the hip. The
doctors were amazed. My bones were so tough nothin' was
broken, but my leg and hip muscles were smashed to ham-
burger.

"The doctors gave me special exercises, and gradually
the strength began to come back, but I had to quit the waterfront.

"At first I got a job with a construction outfit, buildin'
cement forms. I didn't have to use my leg much, just
enough to go and pick up a board and a nail. Later on I
was able to do boom work; I really understand pushin' logs
around in the water. I was very thankful, for in those years
white people, let alone Indians, had terrible trouble gettin'
jobs."

We had come several miles on the return journey from
Cultus Lake, and I turned into a filling station.

"Do you want your free glasses?" asked the pump at-
tendant. When I replied, "No thanks," Dan reached across
and said, "I'll take them. The children break so many."

I'm no longer surprised when I see his jeweled fingers
carefully wrap up half a sandwich or a piece of toast after a
restaurant meal. Tucking it into his pocket, "I'll eat that

later," he'll say, while other diners leave behind them half-filled plates. The lessons of conservation and poverty die hard.

Watching him fold the free glasses carefully in his buckskin jacket, I thought of the anthropology student who had called one day.

"I'm doing this paper on Chief Dan George, and my prof said you might help me."

The young man then asked a number of basic questions that could have been answered by even a cursory glance at newspaper files. Then, "What were his leisure-time activities . . . like . . . uh . . . what were his hobbies as a young man?"

I inquired whether he had checked such a question with his professor.

"Yeah. Sure."

"Well, I suggest you check it again. But the answer is 'survival.' "

The encounter with cultural blindness is a continuing one, and it manifests itself most frequently in those people who are totally unable to conceive of a successful Indian. *To be a success you gotta be white!*

Such people invariably address Dan as though he were not an Indian. Earlier in the day, we had met a longshore-man who'd been brought up in Saskatchewan, and who told us a lot about Indians.

"We always steered clear of them Indians. We were always told, 'Don't go near them.' And we never did—not without a club or a stick.

"An' y'know, Chief, they lit their fires with sticks. Used to rub 'em together—like this." He demonstrated with his knife and fork. "They'd camp all along the railway and the prairie roads—open roads, y'know. And they'd come to our rodeos in their tepees—thirty or forty tepees—and they'd win everything. Yeah. They were real athletic Indians. Different, though—tall—not like our Indians out here."

He paused, then: "Whaddaya think, Chief? I wonder what ever happened to all them Indians?"

Dan emerged from retreat into what Nahanee aptly calls "our big dumb Indian look."

"That," he said, "is a good question."

TEN

IGNORANCE
IN ACTION

We are grateful to the authorities of the Matsqui Institution for allowing us access to the outside world, and for letting us explore our resources without prison supervision.

It is under the auspices of this mutual trust that we speak to you—wishing to share with you a knowledge of our heritage and of our love for the yet unborn children.

—Program notes for Windigo

Dan and his family group have spent much time entertaining in B.C. prisons, and in the years of his success Dan has felt one of his primary obligations to be the visiting and encouragement of Indian prisoners.

After one of his many performances at the B.C. Penitentiary, Dan had been made an Honorary Con for Life by the grateful inmates, and on the occasion of the *Windigo* performance, he was invited as guest of honor.

Windigo is a dramatization of a series of poems by Cam Hubert which deal with aspects of the contemporary Indian world. Ms. Hubert is a poet and playwright living on Vancouver Island who has been involved with native peoples for much of her life. A friend in the United Native Club, an organization of prison inmates, suggested the

work, and permission was received from prison authorities
to allow members of the club to take part in the show.
These greatly gifted inmates not only took on their first
acting roles but created and performed original music for
drums, flute, and guitar.

The occasion disturbed Dan terribly. Usually a fine performance is cause for celebration. But on this night the
greater the talent of the prisoner-performer, the more
poignant was the awareness of the tragic waste of human
creativity.

Under the guidance of professional director Hagan
Beggs, the work was given added impact by the inclusion of
a short, jolting film, *The Ballad of Crowfoot*.

During the film, which he had not seen before, Dan
gripped his hands together until the knuckles whitened,
and sharp intakes of breath revealed his shock at the visual
actuality of the history of his Prairie brothers.

Throughout the damning footage, composer-director
Willie Dunn's "Ballad of Crowfoot" beats as unrelentingly
as a tribal drum.

> Crowfoot, Crowfoot, why the tears?
> You've been a good man for forty years.
> Why the heartache? Why the sorrow?
> Maybe there'll be a better tomorrow.

Based entirely on authentic photographs and sketches
taken from archival records, the National Film Board production depicts the deliberate and unrelenting attempt to
wipe out the North American Indian, and the total massacre of the buffalo herds, on which the Plains Indians de-
pended for life itself.

Crowfoot, recorded in white history books as a wise and noble leader of the Blackfoot, has become yet another controversial figure in contemporary Indian eyes. When Sitting Bull and five thousand of his followers crossed into Canada after the Battle of Little Big Horn, they appealed to Crowfoot, as leader of the most powerful of the northern tribes, to support them in their war of survival. Crowfoot refused, on the basis of his peaceful relationship with "the Great White Mother" (Queen Victoria) and the "Redcoats" (the Northwest Mounted Police).

Today, Crowfoot is considered by many of the young and militant to be the equivalent of a wartime collaborator. They see his descendants still seeking the "better tomorrow" not as proud leaders but as criminals, victims of a justice system they cannot comprehend. Dan frequently appears in court to give support to young Indians who, in their desperate struggle to escape cultural schizophrenia, fall into habits of drugs and alcohol, then inevitably into crime, in order to support those habits. (It is estimated that 80 percent of all native crimes are alcohol-related.)

Once Indians experience prison, many do not wish to leave. A study by the Canadian Criminology and Corrections Association concludes that Indians adapt to prison "as though it were designed for them." When forced back to freedom, they break the law in order to get back "inside," where materially life is much better for them and where they do not feel socially ostracized as they do on the "outside."

After the show Dan met the *Windigo* performers.

There was Sandy, whose fine music, opening gently on guitar, developed a controlled violence that seemed to have nothing to do with the impression of a courteous, handsome youth, and everything to do with his sentence for armed robbery.

There was Brownie, a joyous firecracker of a man, so charged with energy he seemed scarcely to touch the ground. A habitual criminal and as such, under Canadian law, imprisoned for life.

There was Arthur, a giant of warmth and laughter, who leaned over us like a great menacing bird with a single talon—the steel hook that had replaced his missing left hand. In for armed robbery.

There was Ginger, the drummer. Armed robbery.

And Ronnie, the poet. Champion athlete of the prison, lithe, slender, with hair that gleamed like dark rain. Armed robbery.

All twelve of the performers were highly intelligent; some were brilliant. All were dropouts from the white education system, and nearly all were addicted to hard drugs—their one infallible escape from a world that denies both status and identity.

Ronnie, who says, "Poetry comes not from grammar, but from the gut," draws from his Indian imagery to express, as well as he can in his elementary-school English, the infernal circle of the hard-core addict.

The Tracker

Through the night   he walked   alone and lame
A wounded hunter   stalking game

Weary and stumbling   down he fell
Knowing the pain of the coming hell

Exhausted   helpless   in despair
He moaned   and thought   to perish there

But through the gloom a presence smiled
A kindly voice said "Rise my child

Take my spear of shining steel
And rise above the pain you feel

Take this tiny flake of snow
And lonely hunter you will know

The soothing joy that drives away
The cold death of this winter day"

He took the spear and pierced the vein
Soon summer banished winter's pain

But he the hunter then became
The hunted as the tracker found his game

In the months following *Windigo*, I read many of Ronnie's simple, agonized poems about prison life. "Bars! *Bars!*
BARS!" they cried. Yet by the time he was twenty-eight,
Ronnie was so institutionalized that on his last parole he
stole a car outside the prison, presumably so that he would
be back inside in record time. Prison was the only security
he had ever known—the only identity.

The burden of such cases weighs heavily on Dan, for so
many of his own kin have been doomed to prison existence
or have ended brief and tortured lives in suicide.

In British Columbia there are an estimated 115,000 Indians. There is 1 native judge, 6 native lawyers.

Sixty percent of the native population is under twenty-
one, which means that approximately 69,000 are eligible
for education. Only 20,000 are enrolled in the school system. Among these, the level of expectation is appallingly
low, so much so that in 1975 the graduation of eleven na-

tive Canadians from B.C. universities was considered a major news event by the plucky little Indian newspaper, *The Native Voice.*

These students are still experiencing an education system that is completely anti-Indian, even though it is designed in full knowledge of the menticide that has taken place for over a hundred years.

Dan George shares with all Indians the conviction that a primary need of his people is the need for native teachers. Even today, in parts of Canada, native children are forbidden their language, or discouraged from its use. Yet language is the most important link with their culture, their identity, *their parents and grandparents.* They are forced into English, as Dan was, and even then what little they learn is unrelated to their values, although for the urban Indian it is easier.

But how does a child whose life is concerned with his natural environment—fishing, trapping, hunting, survival—relate to textbook stories of buildings, elevators, and supermarkets? The technological concepts are beyond him, and he will never encounter them in his own reality.

Dan George points out that even if an Indian child does conquer the language, he has the great reward of reading history books portraying his people as treacherous and savage, very much as they are depicted in American Western films. Soon his marvelous young energy is drained off in confusion and despair, and the leadership qualities so often developed in wilderness living are destroyed.

A few years ago, "experiments" were made in Canada in which Indian and Eskimo people might take a year of teacher training and then go out and teach in their own tongue. (Denmark and other countries have had similar

programs for a quarter of a century, and at least a dozen reports have been issued by UNESCO to prove what native
people the world over have always known, that a child
learns anything faster if taught *in his native tongue.*)

In the initial year of the experiment, a young teacher
taught her first class of four science students in the Dogrib
tongue. Word went out, and the next day *thirty* students
appeared in the classroom. *It was the first time in their
lives that they had properly understood the teacher.*

Yet at the same time, considerable pressure was placed
on the government by self-interested professionals who
claimed that the Native Teachers Program should be ter-
minated because the candidates "didn't have the proper
credentials"—the university degree that is as ludicrously re-
dundant in such circumstances as a home economics degree for a mother who wants to learn to feed her child. By
the time she qualified, the child would be dead of malnu-
trition.

After the education system, the native is confronted by
the legal system, which for him is merely an extension of
the first; more complex in power and structure and equally
indifferent to his philosophy and mores.

Like many Indians, Dan George recognizes the hope-
lessness of a legal system based entirely on white values,
which few Indians comprehend and in which fewer are involved, and he sees with pain the long battle that must be
fought to bring about change. He believes that we need native administrators of the justice system. We need native
probation officers, not university-trained products of the
white middle class. We need Indian law officers and policemen. Some tribes, such as the Lummi Islanders of the state

of Washington, have their own tribal police force, a vast improvement over the conventional system.

Dan's feelings are echoed by at least one white Canadian law officer, who has shown his concern. Judge Ian Dubienski, of Winnipeg, Manitoba, is a circuit judge working north of the fifty-third parallel. In 1973, after years of concern and of probing into the reasons for Indian confusion regarding white law, Judge Dubienski called a conference of northern Indians, who met with members of the Manitoba Society of Criminology. Members of that conference were unanimous in their conclusion that "the entire system has to be reassessed, and considered anew from an entirely different point of view."

Judge Dubienski quotes two examples from his experience.

"One Indian who appeared before me points up the problem of interpretation. I asked him if he was guilty or not guilty. He didn't answer the question. Instead, through an interpreter, he asked, 'Do I have time to pay?' This man, like most of his brothers, was conditioned to the belief that if a policeman arrested someone, that person must automatically be guilty in the white man's law. All he wanted to know was whether the court would give him time to pay the fine."

In so many cases the alternative is jail, and because Indians do not hoard money—one of the reasons why the native portion of the inmate population is so large—they end up in jail. Another reason is that in police terms, convictions mean promotion. And as ex-RCMP Corporal Jack Ramsay revealed in his 1972 article in *Maclean's Magazine*, "The easiest pinch for statistics is the Indian."

Judge Dubienski brings up another important point: the

effectiveness of our justice system in actually deterring crime.

"When one young Cree returned to his band after a jail term in southern Canada, he was bombarded with questions from his friends. Where had he gone? What was it like?

" 'It was a big building,' an interpreter quoted him as saying. 'There were many people. Everybody was very nice. There was plenty of good food. But they haven't paid my wages yet.' "

"Incredible as it may sound," says Dubienski, "this man had no idea of what was happening. He hadn't understood why he had been arrested and he had not grasped the meaning of jail, which to him was inconceivable. He enjoyed the experience in white man's land, but never really knew what it was about until he got home. He simply figured the white man had needed him in the city and, quite rightly in this context, had expected to be paid for his time."

Such expressions of concern and understanding are rare. In the main, indifference prevails. Chief Dan consciously uses the power that the white man's success-image has given him to make the Indian dilemma more widely known. In doing so he frequently earns the bitter resentment of law officers who continue to mouth platitudes, because he reveals their ignorance and unconcern.

On one occasion, Dan was invited by a member of a coroner's jury to appear as an expert witness in the alleged homicide of an Indian woman. (Like Rita Joe and hundreds of others, she was beaten to death on Vancouver's Skid Road.) The concerned juror apparently felt that someone should be present to speak advisedly on the reasons why cases of this kind occur so frequently.

In his way, which is at once so simple and so eloquent, Dan put forth his plea for an approach to education that might give Indian youth a chance for self-respect and a place in the world. He called on the existing agencies of social and educational welfare to combine with the B.C. Council of Chiefs to find ways of upgrading Indian education.

"Any employer," he said, "can refuse to hire an Indian who is not skilled. But he cannot refuse those who are qualified.

"Where is a girl who comes to the city without education going to find her way?

"Certainly we want to succeed. *But we cannot succeed on your terms.*

"We did not have time to take your twentieth-century 'progress' and digest it, little by little. It was force-feeding all the way, and our stomachs turned sick. We need specialized help *in the formative years*—special courses in English and in guidance counseling.

"Let no one forget it. We are special people, with special rights guaranteed us by promises and treaties. We do not beg for these rights. Nor do we thank you. For we have paid an exorbitant price, as this woman today has paid."

In a reply Stewart McMorran, the city prosecutor on the case, objected to the Chief's "implication" that white men are to blame for the Indians' plight.

"There is nothing to prevent Indians from furthering their education at the present time," he intoned, in a statement that would be questionable coming from an ill-ad-

Dan in his role as the father in the Royal Winnipeg Ballet's production of
The Ecstasy of Rita Joe, 1971. *(Royal Winnipeg Ballet)*

Dan receiving his Honorary Doctor of Laws degree at Simon Fraser University, 1972. *(Tony Westman)*

Listening to speeches of
Canadian brotherhood...
(Tony Westman)

...and receiving their
plaudits. *(Tony Westman)*

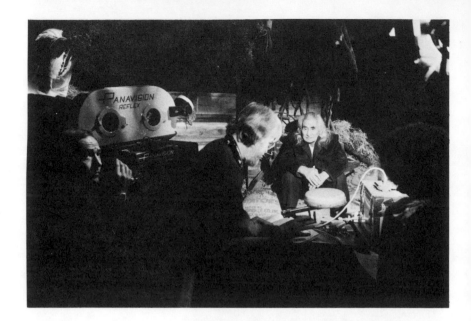

With Canadian director Daryl Duke during shooting of *Shadow of the Hawk*, 1976. *(Tony Westman)*

As Chief Peter A-Tas-Ka-Nay in *The Bears and I*, a Walt Disney production which also starred Patrick Wayne and Michael Ansara. (© *Walt Disney Productions)*

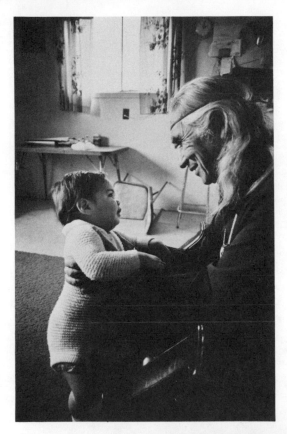

With youngest grandson, Reuben, in living room of the old house. *(Tony Westman)*

Front room of the little house, which remains unchanged by Dan's success, except for the growing collection of portraits by West Coast painters. *(Tony Westman)*

The war canoe log. *(Tony Westman)*

Examining the war canoe for damage to be repaired before spring training begins. *(Tony Westman)*

Dan looking out to sea. Rose's house is on the right. *(Tony Westman)*

vised layman, let alone from a law officer continually dealing with Indian cases.

"There are many avenues of assistance available to
them, from university bursaries to Department of Education scholarships." McMorran added that he believes the
Indians have been given "too much" in the way of reserves
and financial assistance.

"If you give people too much," he parroted in conclusion, "they don't have anything to strive for."

Lip service was paid to Dan's assertions by the coroner's
jury: "The jurors recommend that every effort be made to
carry out Chief Dan's suggestions."

And that is the end of it.

It is a tribute to the tenacity of an old man's spirit that
Dan continues to expose himself to this cultural blindness
again and again, especially since, from the time of his public acclaim, he has been so blatantly exploited by similar
mentalities.

A typical example is a tour arranged for him by a Canadian "brotherhood" organization of well-to-do businessmen. On a hectic cross-country trip, Dan gave nineteen
speeches in eleven days, traveling over five thousand miles.
For this he received no fee, although his expenses were
paid. Another Canadian businessmen's group invited him
to address their convention in Hawaii, again without fee
and without even a day of rest in the sun.

On these occasions, the response of the audience is that
of a mass confessional; having listened and outwardly ac-
knowledged shame for the history of their kind, they ask to
be blessed by his handshake or his autograph, and they feel
absolved.

When I asked him why he consented to these grueling

engagements he replied bitterly, "Because those people are the most ignorant of all. They don't know nothin'. And they don't want to. But they're goin' to be told somethin', whether they like it or not!"

Yet if Dan George's character and energy have done little to change white attitudes, his many public declarations have been of tremendous support to the new courage and determination developing in his own people.

ELEVEN

"PECULIAR ENCOUNTER" OF FRED QUILT

The notorious Fred Quilt case was followed with passionate interest by all Canadians, including Chief Dan. Like most court cases involving native people, this one hit bottom and then, surprisingly, bounced back.

On the freezing night of November 28, 1971, a Chilcotin Indian, Fred Quilt, of the Stone Indian Reserve, had what was called by the committee that later investigated the case "a peculiar encounter" with the Royal Canadian Mounted Police. Returning with his wife Christine and her son Robbin from a funeral, which in Indian country is inevitably followed by the equivalent of an Irish wake, Fred Quilt turned off a wrong exit onto the Chilcotin Road, where his truck engine failed. Like any other travelers along that wilderness route, the Quilts settled down to wait for help to come along. As anyone knows who has experienced that or any similar road in November weather, it's the only thing to do, drunk or sober.

The bizarre events that followed, and which resulted in the excruciating death of Fred Quilt, appeared three weeks later in a top headline story in the Vancouver *Sun* newspaper. The report, in essence, said that while the Quilts were sleeping in their truck, an RCMP vehicle drew up, and a uniformed policeman threw open the door of the truck and dragged Fred Quilt to the ground. Another RCMP, off duty and out of uniform, allegedly began screaming obscenities at Quilt. Without provocation, he "jumped up and down" on the Indian, repeatedly attacking the groin, chest, and head. He wore heavy Western boots, sharp-toed and sharp-heeled.

The members of Quilt's family were then removed to the police truck, where Quilt sat doubled over, bleeding and in agony. Laughing, the two policemen drove the Quilts back to the Reserve where they had attended the funeral, though the RCMP knew them to be from the Stone Reserve just fifteen miles away. They dumped Fred Quilt, still bleeding and moaning in pain, out into the snow in front of the church. Friends helped to get Quilt into their house. They also drove immediately out to the road to rescue Quilt's truck. They found it rolled thirty-five feet off the road and in flames. A red wrapper from a highway flare lay close by.

For two nightmarish days Quilt lay in agony, victim not only of indifference and ineptness on the part of both magistrates and medical officials, to whom his wife appealed in vain through an interpreter, but victim also of his own tribal superstitions. By the time his festering body reached the Williams Lake hospital facilities seventy-five miles away, Quilt had only an hour and twenty minutes to live.

In mid-January of 1972 a three-day inquest was held in Williams Lake, the prosperous cattle town from which the Chilcotin Road makes its tortuous way through vast plateau and river canyon, westward to the Pacific.

Chief Dan noted at the time that RCMP witnesses were subpoenaed and their expenses paid to attend the proceedings (including Constable Bakewell and his companion in the incident, Constable Eakins). He also noted that no Indians were invited or subpoenaed to the first inquest, not even Quilt's wife Christine or her son Robbin, the only witnesses to the affair. They hitchhiked their way to Williams Lake and paid their own expenses.

The autopsy on Fred Quilt was performed by Dr. Han Choo Lee, a surgeon of twelve years' experience. He gave the cause of death as peritonitis, the result of a severed small intestine that could only have been caused by a sharp external blow, probably a kick, in the lower right abdomen. He further testified that this injury occurred approximately forty-eight hours prior to death, at about the time Quilt was being assisted to the police vehicle by Constable Daryl Bakewell. Han Choo Lee also stated that surgery within twelve hours could certainly have saved Quilt's life.

At a later inquest, doubt was thrown on the doctor's testimony when an RCMP pathologist suggested that Han Choo Lee himself might have severed the intestine "during a hurried autopsy," thus raising the question of how peritonitis developed *after death*. Another medical man testifying for the RCMP, Dr. Clem Martin, of Kamloops, expressed his opinion that appendicitis had caused the peritonitis.

The second inquest was held because, for once in Canadian history, the Indian people refused to accept either the RCMP story or the jury's verdict, which read:

> We find that Frederick Quilt of the Stone Reserve, aged 55 years, died on the 30th of November AD 1971 as a result of peritonitis. We find this death was unnatural and that it was accidental. We attach no blame to any person in connection with the death.

The verdict was no surprise. An RCMP constable, Daryl Bakewell, was alleged to have beaten Quilt to death. The investigation was carried out by an RCMP friend and senior officer of Bakewell. The inquest was held before a retired member of the RCMP, now a coroner. Instead of that coroner calling the jury in the first place, it was chosen by the RCMP detachment at Williams Lake. Not only was it an all-white, all-male jury; one juror lived in a house with two RCM policemen, and the jury foreman was an auxiliary RCM policeman.

A month after this fiasco, a Fred Quilt Committee was formed in Vancouver. Supported by churches, unions, social work organizations, the newspapers, and even members of the legislature, the committee demanded not only that a new inquest be held but that charges be laid against Constable Bakewell. Throughout the province posters appeared:

JOIN THE RCMP AND KILL AN INDIAN!

Following the November incident, the professional career of Constable Daryl Bakewell had been slowly emerging in a very murky light. His record showed twice the normal number of transfers, and in each case the transfer was accompanied by suggestions of violence, allegedly in cases of Indians who were drunk, who did not speak English, and who were alone. There appeared to be some doubt that he actually had pistol-whipped a handcuffed fourteen-year-old Indian boy just before transfer from his last detachment, but there was no doubt that when a reporter for the *Native Voice* (a native Indian) asked a professional question about the Quilt case, Bakewell grabbed him by the shirt and offered to break his nose.

Less than a week later, in conversation with the schoolteacher on the Stone Reserve, Bakewell demonstrated how he would "teach these Indians to tell the truth" by making the motions of clubbing them over the head. Alan Haig-Brown, the cool and respected white teacher, was later approached by RCMP lawyers to act as a character witness for Bakewell. He refused, saying that he would prefer to be such a witness for the Indian people.

Pressure by the Quilt Committee at first brought only token reaction from B.C.'s Attorney-General, Leslie Peterson, who merely directed the chief coroner to review the evidence at the first inquest. This political expediency did not appease the committee. When the Civil Liberties Union also joined the action, and when the Chairman of the Legal Committee of the Human Rights Council defined the attitude of the original jury as "paternal racism," Peterson was forced to call a new inquest.

I asked Dan if he would like to attend, since there seemed to be some optimism that this milestone in legal history might bring about a fairer investigation. But he replied sadly, "No. No. It went against us before. It will go against us again. It always goes against us. And I do not wish to be there."

He was right. The second jury, chosen by ballot, was mostly merchants and businessmen, a group unlikely to challenge law enforcement officers in any context.

The waffling verdict read:

We find that death was caused by peritonitis of the abdomen over a 48-hour period, caused by perforation of the small bowel. The perforation was the result of an injury by way of an unknown blunt object to the lower right abdomen.

The injury was sustained between the time

Quilt was removed from the Quilts' vehicle and assisted to the police vehicle on the Chilcotin Road on November 28. *Due to the unwillingness of Quilt to avail himself of medical aid that was available to him*, Quilt's activities during this period of the day, the modes of transportation, the conditions of the road and the lapse of time were contributing factors [emphasis added].

The question of who set fire to the Quilt truck was never investigated, and no charges were laid against Constable Bakewell.

Harry Rankin, the militant Vancouver lawyer who handled the case for the estate of Fred Quilt, said:

So we're asked to believe that an unknown force severed a man's bowel. Deep within our system is an inherent prejudice. It's very much like the logic of RCMP medical experts. They couldn't believe, in spite of the testimony, that an RCMP would jump on a man. Therefore the man couldn't have been injured and the bowel, Q.E.D., was not severed.

He added that there was little chance of charges ever being laid against Bakewell.

"Due to the unwillingness of Quilt to avail himself of medical aid . . ."

This statement refers to the fact that an ambulance arrived twenty-four hours after Quilt was injured. The ambulance carried the body of a dead child. According to Chilcotin belief, those who journey with the dead will join them the following day, and Fred Quilt, already so close to death, refused to go in the ambulance. By the time it returned for him at one o'clock the next day, his life was running out.

During both inquests, traditions of the Indians complicated the proceedings. Many Chilcotins will not speak a man's name within a year of his death, convinced that it will bring him back from his rest. This reluctance of many witnesses to speak Fred Quilt's name in the courtroom caused much laughter among the whites present.

According to another tradition among older Indian women, it is considered presumptuous to look directly into a man's eyes. Christine Quilt, the modest lady who was Fred's wife, devoted to him and their four adopted children, is one of those traditional women. Yet the lawyer for the RCMP tried continuously and sadistically to force Christine to look at him. Through an interpreter he implied in accepted WASP fashion that if "you cannot look me in the eye," you have something to hide.

"Christine, I wonder if you could look at me when you're answering," he said. "Kindly look at me so I can see your eyes. This is a very important matter we are here on today."

(Only her husband's death.)

Later, to the interpreter: "Have her look at me!"

This patronizing attitude is found not only in the courts of the nation but pervades every government department, including Education and Indian Affairs.

How many times in his long life has Dan George seen the same charade played out? "It always goes against us. And I do not wish to be there."

And he was right. The usual "recommendation" was made, of course: "That assistance be given to ethnic minority groups in their dealings with the courts."

In his summing up, Harry Rankin felt that something had been achieved. "The fighting of the Quilt case will make life a hundred times easier for the Indians. Brutal racist police will realize they can't move the Indians so easily. They know they're being watched."

They know. But nothing in our justice system as it applies to Indians says they have to care.

TWELVE

THE REBELLION
AT DUCK LAKE

The production brochure for the film read:

  History, action, romance in the Canadian West will
be the main fare of *Alien Thunder*, starring Donald
Sutherland and Chief Dan George, to be shot in Saskatchewan between August 15 and October 30, 1972.
  Because of the inherent dramatic qualities of the
story, *Alien Thunder* will be an unusual Western.

It was.
First of all there was the crew, mostly Québecois, mostly
urban Montrealers.
Then there were the Cree.
Then there were the RCMP.
And the rest: Dan, Lennie, Susan, assorted bit players,
and the star, Donald Sutherland, with his nutty little dog
MacNicol and his equally nutty Cockney companion-
chauffeur.
  Throw in a self-styled medicine man who looked like an
encyclopedia salesman, put them all together in one of the
bleakest motels and ill-equipped film sets imaginable, and
yes . . . the brochure says it . . . we had all the inherent
dramatic qualities of an unusual Western; on set and off.
  The stars were great; the technicians, top professionals.
  The RCMP were very good at riding.

The Cree were very good at sitting.

The directors were something else. Especially as there were two of them, Claude Fournier of Onyx Films and his lady, Marie-José Raymond, doing her first major directing job on the second unit.[1]

Some of the French crew didn't speak English.

Some of the English crew didn't speak French.

And some of the Cree spoke neither.

So we had two directors trying to overcome three language barriers, with large numbers of people who had never been on a set before.

Dan and I joked about smoke signals—appropriate and quiet—but the grass was too dry for a fire. It would only have blown into a prairie fire. And there were enough people burning up already.

The film was being shot in two major locations, one near the small town of Duck Lake, Saskatchewan, fifty miles north of Saskatoon, the other a few miles away on a high, golden bluff sweeping down to a dense copse of birch trees.

Since the film unit was housed near Saskatoon, this meant many miles of driving each day, adding to an already grueling and disorganized schedule.

The story of *Alien Thunder* was taken from the RCMP case files of 1895, ten years after the Northwest Rebellion at Duck Lake,[2] and was designed to commemorate the one-hundredth anniversary of the police force.

All the elements of a fine film were there; it was an authentic, classic story of the tragedies that follow in the wake of cultural surgery.

Almighty Voice,[3] a gifted young Cree leader, is arrested with his brother for shooting an unbranded cow. He is placed in irons by Sergeant Colebrooke of the RCMP who, with the cultural arrogance and rigid by-the-rules outlook typical of his breed ("I was only carrying out orders") admits no need for meat in the cruel Saskatchewan winter of 1895.

A fellow officer, Sergeant Trumper, loosens the leg-irons to enable the prisoners to sleep, and Almighty Voice escapes. Colebrooke sets out to recapture him and, disregarding the Cree's warning as he approaches, is shot.

Trumper is demoted for negligence, and sets out to avenge Colebrooke's death.

The chase lasts for almost two years, ending in the little copse at the bottom of the bluff, where Almighty Voice, his brother, and his brother-in-law are surrounded by 150 lion-hearted RCMP with their friends and blasted to death by cannon fire.

The key role of Sergeant Trumper was played by Donald Sutherland. Dan was Chief Sounding Sky, father of Almighty Voice. Lennie played Almighty Voice's brother, and Gordon Tootoosis, a tall, stunningly handsome Cree, was Almighty Voice. Tootoosis is a natural performer, for he is famous as one of the great traditional dancers and drummers of his nation.

The young fugitive's wife was played by Ernestine, an exquisite sixteen-year-old Cree, and among many Indians engaged as extras and for smaller parts was Sarain Stump, the gifted Shoshone poet and artist.[4]

The film had been under way for several weeks when I arrived, hoping to write about Dan's glamorous life as a film star on location. It was a cold October day, and I found the set seething with tension.

I learned that Lennie, wise in the ways of film and union

regulations, had just confronted the directors on behalf of the rebellious Indians.

Until his entrance on the scene, they appear to have been underpaid, undersheltered, underinsured, and overexploited due to the prevailing attitude that labels all Indians "a bunch of stupid Indians."

The final crisis had developed during an escape scene in which Ernestine, approached by Gordon on horseback, was lifted into the saddle at full gallop. Even with a trick horse, this is a dangerous procedure for an untrained girl.

The scene had to be reshot eight times. In spite of her terror, Ernestine's natural reflexes carried her through beautifully, as we saw later when screening the rushes.

But when Lennie discovered that Ernestine had no contract, was not insured or even receiving risk pay, he took the accumulated grievances of many days to the film management.

"What really built up in my head," Lennie told me, "was their total lack of understanding of us as actors. It was like they had an *idea of Indians* and we were *Indians*. We couldn't be Indians and actors. They just couldn't get it together.

"Gordon and I were doing our first major roles. We wanted to do our best—to have some rapport with the directors and discuss interpretation, our impressions of the roles, and the script.

"But they put off meeting with us again and again.

"Then they'd discuss the whole scene in French, on the set, and just say, 'Okay. I want *you* here. Do this and do it now.'

"And they herded the Indians around like they were shit. They never thought of them as human, even the old ladies. There was no thought for their comfort, like trying to get them into the bus first, or having someone to look after them and interpret for those who couldn't speak English.

"Even Dan, because he was an Indian, was just shoved on the bus with all the extras, and he'd be up on the bluff all day in that freezing cold, doing nothing. He didn't even have a changing room. He was just hassled around in the wardrobe room with all the others.

"There was never any feeling for an actor's need for privacy, for silence before his next scene.

"Food was brought up hours too early, so everything got cold. People got ptomaine poisoning, and eventually I blew. I told Fournier, 'The only progress in this film since films were made about Indians is that you're using Indians in Indian parts. Otherwise you haven't moved any farther than The Lone Ranger and Tonto. You had a beautiful story here, and you missed the whole thing. All you've done is whitewash the RCMP.'

"Donald Sutherland was disgusted. When he signed his contract, he specified that all the Indians in the cast must be Indians. He'd said, 'If I'm going to play an RCMP officer, I'm not going out and chase some white Indians through those hills.'

"Whatever quality the film had certainly came from Donald. Of course, if we'd been able to conceive of such directors, we'd have had plenty written into our contracts too."

Under pressure from Lennie and Gordon, a few improvements were made. Eventually Dan got his own small trailer and a semiprivate car in which he was driven to the locations, supposedly only when he was required on set.

Some of the Indian contracts were revised, but there seemed no real concern for the group in general.

Not only the Indians but the crew were disgruntled. The film unit had been living for weeks in a dismal motel twelve miles from Saskatoon—two stories of gray concrete block surrounded by iron railings. Dust from the freeway blew constantly across the blacktop parking lot, seeping into what little was edible in the bleak coffee shop attached to the motel.

This was the only source of food for several miles, except for the film unit commissary, which could not always be brought back from location in time to supply Donald Sutherland's vegetarian tastes and the Québecois thirst for Vichy water.

Many of the crew had never been west of Quebec or Ontario; some had worked only in studio locations in Montreal. Nearly all were suffering culture shock and professional ennui, the causes of which began to appear as I watched the following day's shooting.

Location: Duck Lake.

Scene: Treaty Day.

Indian Affairs officials are due to arrive to distribute Queen Victoria's bounty of ten dollars per annum per Indian. The little town—trading post, RCMP barracks, small stores—has been set up along a rutted dirt road already frozen hard. There is a section of track on which a noble old steam train, circa 1882, will play its role later in the film.

Settlers' wagons are dragged on set. Napoleon, the wrangler, brings in his train of Indian horses, tying them behind the trading post, well out of camera range.

Fournier, Raymond, and camera artist Michel Brault[5] are setting up the first shots.

Two hours later they are still setting up. Interminable conferences take place in French. At last, after some rapid-fire instructions in English to the waiting Indians, Brault begins to shoot the arrivals at the Treaty Day rendezvous in the trading post.

Among them are Chief Sounding Sky (Dan) and his wife, played by Gordon Tootoosis' mother-in-law, who speaks only Cree.

Things are not going well.

The horses, spooked by unfamiliar sounds and the monster eye of the three-legged camera, balk continually and swerve out of shooting range.

No effort seems to have been made to cross the language barrier in order to give the Cree adequate direction. They're expected to get it by osmosis—and *do it now*.

Fournier takes the camera. He seems to feel that if he gets behind the lens, everything will all come together. It doesn't, of course, and even before the opening scene is shot, it's lunch break.

Everyone heads for the ancient train, now being stoked up for a trial run. Dan is invited to take the controls and with the delight of a small boy, he chugs us all up and down the track. The engineer asks him to autograph his hat, then hangs it in the place of honor over the coal burner.

"There!" he says with satisfaction. "That's one that'll go up on the peg and never come down."

After lunch everyone not needed on the set is herded into the cramped rear quarters of the trading post.

The Québecois remain aloof from the Indians. When I speak with one of the Cree or with Sarain Stump about his art, I can feel their conditioned contempt, quite unmixed with curiosity.

It is bitterly cold, even indoors. Since there's no way out through the front of the store, where they're shooting, some of the Cree exit by the window and take turns galloping the horses to keep warm. Finally Dan and I take the same route and, only a few hundred yards from the false-fronted film set, find ourselves on the outermost rim of the world.

The harvest is up.

Chaff, palomino pale, gilds the land and invades the air. The bitter wind is persistent, unremitting as a mistral.

Golden grasses throw ribbons of light from marsh and lake edge. Miles of bulrush lanterns explode their seeds like white fire in a world of light so total, the rare shape of house or haystack seems an illusion—a hard-edge mirage doubled and redoubled on the shimmering air.

The mind-consuming light blots out time.

I feel I'm merging into space, where only the dry reeds whisper their secret legends.

I have never felt so profoundly the spirit range of the Indian.

Dan says it's time to go in for his next scene, to be enacted in the storefront of the trading post. Chief Sounding Sky and his wife are spending the Queen's money buying white man's goods. Dan is pointing out the strange objects to his wife.

From behind the camera, Fournier calls out, "Chief! When you are shoppeeng, I wan' you to whisper to 'er."

They begin again, Dan speaking gently in English.

"*Non!* I don' wan' you to whisper to 'er in English. I wan' you to whisper to 'er in Cree."

Dan looks up. The big, slow grin starts. Someone from the Coast says, "Try whispering to 'er in Salish, Dan. Nobody will know the difference."

He did, and they didn't.

Driving back from location at sunset, I tell Dan about my feeling of being alien, yet so much a part of this mystic landscape.

"I felt that way at first," he replied. "I lost my sense of direction, away from the mountains and the sea. And the light hurt my eyes."

He turned toward the last relentless fires of the sun.

"Here, it's so flat, I think the sun will roll off the edge, right to the bottom of the world."

The next morning when I came out of the breakfast trailer, Lennie handed me a warm brown bundle in minuscule-fringed white buckskin. Susan had arrived from Vancouver the night before with the new baby.

I carried him upstairs to Lennie's room, making love noises into his perfumed dome, just a few weeks old.

A strange voice beside me: "The child is called Flying Eagle. I had this vision . . ."

Lennie said, "This is Jim Thomas. He's a medicine man. He came yesterday."

". . . I had this vision of a great cloud parting and an eagle coming forth . . . and I knew this was the son of my brother. And I have seen the future of my brother's son . . . and he will be a great and powerful leader . . . flying above all his people . . ."

There was no suggestion of flight in the baby's marsupial clutch.

"Great," I thought. "Right now he needs changing."

". . . and when I took this cancer from this woman, I disappeared for three days . . ."

"You mean in limbo?"

". . . I was in another place. That is when my visions come. I saw a great tree . . . many Indians grew from its roots . . . and its leaves became Indian faces. They flowed into thousands of my people moving down a road . . . and I was leading them."

I put Flying Eagle on the bed, to wiggle free and naked after his long confinement in the plane, and now I take a closer look at the visitor.

Short, stocky. He has none of the Cree grace in his body. Close-clipped redneck hair, casual slacks, shirt, and sports jacket. Yellow-stained fingers of the chain smoker.

He could be any traveling salesman. And he certainly talks a lot.

". . . and I could sell my Indian culture for money . . . but God would take the power from me . . ."

He moves like one of those City Indians who so disturbed me in Robert Altman's movie. I fantasy him in all those different costumes, but none of them fit.

He still comes out City Indian.

"Where are you from?"

"I have come from the East . . . like the Wise Men of old, . . ." He butts another cigarette. "And for three days I have fasted to purify my body for my great task . . ."

Maybe he's chain-smoking to cut down his appetite.

". . . and if you will kneel with me I will say a prayer in my own tongue."

He kneels and bows his head. What's he doing down

there? Why doesn't he stand and look directly up to the Great Spirit?

The prayer is lyrical in sound, and he delivers it well, though for all of us here, including Dan, he could be invoking his spirits in Urdu.

I ask him what the words mean.

"I gave thanks to God and asked him to bring honor to my brother, and my brother's son, and to my father the Chief."

His brother's son is munching on his father the Chief's fringed buckskin, and as I pick Flying Eagle up, I wonder whether this sudden uncle has adopted any of the less well-heeled members of the cast.

He speaks of holding a Medicine Lodge far out in the remote countryside. But I get the feeling he'd be more at home outside a circus tent than inside a tepee. He is still talking.

". . . and now I will tell you what I am trying to say to my people . . ."

On and on. Flying Eagle blows bubbles in my ear.

"Blluurrr, blullbullbulll . . ."

Many months later, long after Jim disappeared out of his life as mysteriously as he had come, Lennie told me what happened one night when Flying Eagle got sick.

Susan, weary of controversy and especially of the drunken escapades of Gordon and Lennie, those blood brothers in mischief, had, for the first and last time in her life, got drunk.

No half measures.

She downed a whole bottle of tequila, insulted everyone from the Montreal moneybags to director Fournier, and told Lennie *he* could take care of the baby for a change.

But Flying Eagle didn't cooperate. He got colic.

Lennie, desperate without his native roots and remedies, which had been left at the Coast, paced the floor with a fevered, relentlessly screaming infant.

"Do something!" he appealed to Jim.

Jim undressed Flying Eagle (screaming even harder at this violation by a stranger) and laid his hands on the bulging little belly.

"I will draw the fire from his body through my own."

But the little belly only grew fatter and hotter.

Lennie paced, and the baby screamed, well past midnight, when a completely distraught young father cried, "Jim! What am I going to *do?*"

"For Christ's sake," said the medicine man, "call a doctor!"

On the day after the medicine man's arrival, Sunday, Dan disappeared early in the morning. When he had not returned by noon, a concerned Lennie made inquiries, for it was unusual for Dan to go out alone. No one had accompanied him, and no taxi had been called. In the coffee shop we met the medicine man, who said he had spoken with Dan early that morning, but did not know where he had gone. Two hours later, having been gone six hours, Dan came back, looking more gray and tortured than I had seen him since Amy's death.

"Jim says you spoke with him this morning."

"Yes. I told him some of my problem."

He hesitated, then went on in his slow way:

"I told him how my family is so worried about me. It's all right when I'm workin', but when I stop, my mind is a blank. And then thoughts come into it that will not go away. I know she is waitin' for me, and I do not know what to do."

"And you really think such a medicine man can help you?"

"I do not know. He seems to know somethin' of the old beliefs, but I will have to go slowly with him."

"What did you do all morning?"

"In my confusion, I walked and walked as far as I could, and then I went to Mass."

We joined a worried family in Dan's room, where he turned on the television set. Someone said lightly, "If you watch much more television, you're going to go blind!"

"It keeps me from thinkin'."

"Don't think," I suggested. "Tell us a story."

His face began to relax.

"Did I ever tell you about the serpent at Belcarra?"

"No."

He began.

"At a place called Kapulpaqua, on the inlet where our home once was, there are promontories, very, very steep, on either side.

"Long ago, in the time of my great-great-great-grand-father, a sea serpent came to the inlet. As you know, its waters are very, very deep, for there are mountains under that water, and fathomless valleys. So the serpent was able to swim almost to our home.

"But when he came to Kapulpaqua, he got stuck in that narrow space, only a quarter-mile wide. And he lay there, year after year, with his head up the cliff on one side and his tail climbing the other.

"And there was a legend that whoever passed over his body would die. So my people would take their canoes from the water, carry them over the steep hill, and then continue on to their fishing grounds.

"And this went on for many generations.

"Now my great-great-great-grandmother gave birth to a little boy. She had already many children, but this little fellow seemed special. He was so smart he was even allowed to wander alone, for he was clever enough to find his way home always.

"One autumn morning, a mother seal came to our shores and began calling and crying in her own language. The little boy understood her well, and he went to that mother seal and swam away with her.

"Then the Chief, my great-great-great-grandfather, sent his young braves in their canoes to bring back his son. But whenever they came close, the boy and the seal would dive as one body and escape.

"At last they came to the place we now call Second Narrows, where the inlet flows into the sea. And the braves knew they could not follow into the open gulf.

"So they took arrows and tried to kill that seal. But she was protected by the Great Spirit, and soon the two seemed lost forever.

"Now on that same day, sixteen years later, a young boy was seen on the other side of the inlet, walking toward Belcarra. When darkness came, he swam across the waters to his home and went straight to his sleeping place. For his mother had kept it for him.

"No one questioned him next day—where or why.

"He was just accepted back into the tribe.

"But it came out that he had been chosen by the Great Spirit to be the shaman of the Tsla-a-wat people. At that time we had none, for the old shaman had died, and a visitor from Lillooet, up in the Fraser River Canyon, would come when our people needed help.

"This shaman said to my great-great-great-grandfather, 'You need me no more. You have your shaman.'

"And when the boy found that his people still carried their canoes in fear, his first act was to climb the hill to where the serpent lay. He went straight to the fearful head and took his great stone club and killed the serpent.

"And on both sides of the inlet, you could see his body sliding down into the deep waters.

"And no one saw him ever more.

"And our people rejoiced to go again to their fishing grounds without fear."

Dan seemed relaxed now, as always when he reenters the past. We thanked him for the bedtime story.

"It made me homesick," he said.

On Monday we are on location early, for Gordon Tootoosis' death scene, the death of Almighty Voice, is being shot today.

Sergeant Trumper (Donald Sutherland) is trying to persuade Chief Sounding Sky (Dan) to induce Almighty Voice to surrender.

Sitting all about the bluff are the motionless Cree, costumed in brilliant blankets, in headpieces of porcupine quills and bluebirds' wings. The brushstrokes, red and purple, of buckbrush and blueberry—the tawny orange of wolf willow—seem to etch them forever into the landscape.

All the leaves are blown now, and the black hillside soil, patterned by the harvester, circles from the center field like a sprung reel of film.

Off camera, Ernestine, supple as a small wolf, curls against the cold in a burrow of earth lined with straw from the thresher.

They're having trouble with the scene.

Dan can't seem to remember his lines. The rhythm is all wrong. Sutherland wants to alter one word to make his own lines flow more easily.

This calls for another great conference with both directors. A few more takes and Sutherland, in despair, goes back to the original. I begin to understand why W. O. Mitchell, who did the first adaptation, has refused screen credits for the script.

The dramatic denouement comes when Sounding Sky refuses Trumper's plea to intercede and avoid further bloodshed. Instead, he turns toward the copse where Almighty Voice is hidden and, crying the low, sad death chant of his tribe, extols the virtues of his beloved son, exhorting him to die bravely.

Even in this context, it is deeply moving. It brings tears to the eyes of the costume girl sitting beside me.

"I would not like to be an actor in dis film. Dey don' care a damn about the Indians. De girl, Ann Pritchard, she do all the research, but dey don' ask 'er. Dey don' want to know."

"Why are they so unconcerned?"

"In Québec we are not allowed to know about de Indians. You remember, when the Québec government asked to take over Indian affairs and Indian lands, the Indians said, *'Jamais de la vie!* Already we 'ave the federal government. You wan' to punish us some more?' An' I don' blame them."

"But you're concerned."

"With me it is different. I am from the Manitoulin Island.[6]

"*Quiet on the set!*"

It's an order that rings out over the whole place.

It's a retake.

Again Dan sings his mourning chant. And soaring from the copse comes the answer—the battle cry of the Cree.

The frozen hours of boredom are wiped out.

Nothing has moved, yet the whole bluff seems vibrating. Silver birch trunks, golden slivers of chaff, all are transistor wires carrying Gordon's fearful exultance.

It is microtonic, yet many tones higher than West Coast sound, and so piercing that I feel the frozen air will shatter round me in shards of glass.

My skin prickles in atavistic joy. There is nothing—nothing at all—between this cry and nature herself.

What I have felt *is* real . . . the world *is* vibrating. This is a summons to battle of all the spirits of earth and sky.

"Some nights out 'ere, you can see the stars sing," whispers the costume girl.

The last echo flies.

"Cut!" says the A.D.

Behind us: "*Merde!* Would you believe dis town? Still no Vichy water. Between Montreal and Edmonton, no Vichy water!"

C'est donc de valeur!

No Vichy water at Duck Lake.

Que faites-vous dans cette ville sauvage?

The battle-cry scene is reshot at least six times.

Meanwhile, unseen among the trees of the copse, the special-effects crew has been fusing a dynamite system, the voice of the nine-pound cannon that blows off Almighty

Voice's head. It is timed to go off in an hour and ten minutes, at ten after four.

There's a lot of speculation about what could happen to Gordon. Pierre Dury, the stills photographer, says, "I'm glad it's his head they're holding in their hands, not mine!"

We discuss the previous day's rushes—the lyrical camera work of Michel Brault and the totally unrelated approach of Fournier, who insists on taking over the camera.

"How will they ever match it up?" I wonder.

"*Pas possible,*" says Dury.

Down in the copse, they are still fiddling around with cameras and dynamite. What meager, mongering men they appear beside the tall Cree, who now moves toward the copse. Gordon carries his inherited pride as gracefully as his talent. There is a true sense of place, of self without ego.

"*C'est tout un homme!*" says the costume girl.

Dan comes to join us and, watching Gordon's tall stride, remarks how different it is to hunt and track in this open land, where every sign is etched in the dust, and little shelter found in the sparse stands of slender trees. So unlike tracking in the deep Coastal forests, where rain and the dense, springing undergrowth can quickly obliterate the passage of even large game.

Someone brings a bulletin that the crew has rebelled again, refusing to work with Marie-José in the director's chair.

The wind increases—colder, colder.

Because of the sound, we can't start the car engine to keep warm.

Finally I'm cold enough—and bored enough—to cheat. I

peek at the back of the production book to see where this turgid epic is finally leading our heroes.

And guess what?

Trumper the tracker has decided to sacrifice his career as a professional cop and go into—you guessed it—Indian Affairs.

And that's not all. It looks as though his life companion in this noble work will be none other than the dead constable's French-Canadian wife!

Que ça change?

At last, from the depths, the intercom: "Ees de sound ready?"

"I'm ready, man."

Sardonic, resigned, he has been ready for nine hours.

BoooooOOM!

In a hurricane of wolf willow leaves, Napoleon's horse bolts up the hill.

Gordon, resurrected, emerges from the copse.

"*On est chanceux!*" remarks Dury. "Gordon still has his head on!"

And just before dark, the most welcome words of the day:

"Okay! It's a wrap!"

There is no heat in Dan's small trailer. No light.

The wind is even stronger here on top of the bluff, battering the tin cocoon like a Ping-Pong ball. My hands are so cold. In the near-dark, I'm trying to unlace the leather thongs from Dan's hair.

"Would it help if we worked on your lines?"

"I don't know. I cannot seem to remember."

Since Amy's death, I have never felt so deeply his life weariness.

Poor, tired, famous, bereaved, old man.

But his spirits lighten in the next few days, for his part in the shooting is over; it's time to return to the woods and the sea.

Flight shapes our last look at the prairie, etched in an art form unperceived on the ground.

From the air, we see clearly how some focal point of land, a swamp, a brown water hole, a little rise, both invites and controls the harvester's round. We imagine what it would be to drive a combine in these fields—to trace colossal curves or drive across diagonally, divide the land into grandiose triangles, then fill them all in like a child's coloring book.

Below us now, the man-made patterns recede. And as we rise, the harmonious whole becomes an infinity of Tantric symbols, unfolding in the vast, exultant light.

THIRTEEN

VOYAGEUR

I go early on the water
the way See-see-um watched
and know no more sad stories
of these shores.

For I have grown restless
with the west wind's song at sunset
and my soul is captured
by its lures.

It tells of wild geese crying
and loons' alarms along the lakes
and arias of wolves that
sing to stars.

It leaves me deafened
to the city's pain and fear:
See-see-um's whispered call is
all I hear.[1]

Spring, 1976. A decade ago we sat on this beach below the
Reserve, in the shelter of the great cedar log. It still rests
here, silvered now by ten years' storms; but the years of
fame have given no time for Dan to fulfill his hope of carving from this tree his last war canoe. Like the spirit of his
own talent, which took so many years to mature and

emerge, the spirit of the canoe still lies waiting in the wood, perhaps to be released by one of many grandsons.

He will, after all, be seventy-seven this coming summer.

It is April, and for weeks now we have been watching the young men of the tribe training for the annual war canoe races, held from May to September along the coast of the Pacific Northwest. Training is rigid, and each member of the eleven-man crews must be faithful to that training for at least four months, running miles each morning and evening to temper their supple bodies for the grueling drive across the waters.

Dan recalls that as late as his father's day the preparation for this ordeal was part of daily life, of the sea hunt and the travel from tribe to tribe. Some still perform the ancient rituals—the morning plunge into icy mountain streams, the rubbing of the body with purifying potions—but, Dan says, the young men have changed:

"Their bodies are different now. They sit all day in a schoolroom, or work in white men's conditions, and eat his kind of food. So it takes them much longer to get accustomed to this great test of endurance.

"Once the canoe was a way of life. Now, they only get in it for racin' and trainin'."

Bob George has come to join us. He well remembers his own youthful days of training under the stern eye of a favorite uncle.

"I was up at four-thirty every mornin'. In those days a little mountain crick ran down here, and I'd have to get in that ice water, which came straight down off the high snow. Afterward, I'd rub myself all over with hemlock boughs, like they did in the old days." He laughed. "By the time I got through trainin', I was so tough that when I'd

play with my kids and they'd splash water on me, they'd
say, 'Look at Daddy! He's dead! He can't feel nothin'!' "

Bob and his father are hoping that this year's crew, skip-
pered by Lennie, will regain the championship status they
both achieved earlier in life.

Everyone on Dan's Reserve looks forward to the annual
races, which are not only a thrilling sports event but a great
social celebration—a time of family reunion similar to the
winter feasting of older times, when the Indian's year was
reversed.

Bent now to the white man's way, the Indian works in
winter and plays for a short time in summer. In the time of
natural rhythms, he worked at food-gathering through
spring and summer, played and feasted in the long dark
winters of the western forest.

But the tribes still gather from three hundred miles of
coastline in British Columbia, and across the United States
border into western Washington.

And though ceremonial dress has given way to American
casual and bumper stickers are the symbols of war (CUSTER
DIED IN AN ARROW SHIRT), there is still rich color in the costumes of visiting tribal dancers, in the canoes with their
gleaming, many-colored coats, in the burnished glow of the
cedar's natural gold, and in the bronze grace of powerful
bodies.

The gathering place may be the central beach of some
highly developed community, once an ancient meeting
ground, or it may be a remote stretch of shore, an almost
untouched curve of beach, shoulder-deep in pure white
shell—the patined debris of centuries of feasting birds and
beings.

Here the camps are made, the fires lit, the succulent

food prepared for the two- or three-day meet. Freshly caught salmon, barbecued on wire racks or hung over driftwood smoke; oysters gathered each day from the rich waters and barbecued in the shell or baked in shallow rock pits; fresh clams; and hot Indian bread, shaped by hand on top of a wood stove.

And always there is the sound of the "bone game." In spite of Dan's explanations, I have never been able to follow this ancient gambling ritual, in which two teams of players sit opposite each other, about twenty feet apart. Two marked bones, curved to fit the hollow of a hand, are passed back and forth with many mystic gestures; the trick is to guess, when challenged, who is holding the bones. The spectators bet heavily, chant unceasingly. Dan told me that these songs, or "bone chants," are constantly changing to convey subtle signals and to distract the players. Chanting and drumming pulse through the night, for once begun, the bone game continues uninterrupted for the duration of the meet.

The canoe meets diminish each year as skills and motivation shift, but it is still possible to see twenty or more eleven-man war canoes in the thrilling final race.

Now, in the calm evening light, we watch the training canoes fly across the waters to the shore beyond. A rosy gauze of new alder catkins shrouds the marching oil tanks, and the far hills return the thrilling chant of the paddlers.

"A-HEE a-Hah! A-HEE-a-Hah! Ay-YEEEEEE-HAH!"

As the paddles are switched from one side of the canoe to the other, the chant rises to a high tone, then falls to a kind of keening—a steady, mystical rhythm—as full racing power is gained. With the paddlers, the chant builds to

full strength and harmony, reaching its triumphant peak in
the final victory thrust toward the beach.

They fly swiftly this April evening, for the state of the
sea is quiet, with only gentle, lilting waves to catch the fall-
ing gold of the sun.

More often these are wild and treacherous waters, swirl-
ing with tide rips and secret currents. A canoe can be
swamped in seconds, and in these icy seas the survival rate
of a man under extreme exertion is brief indeed.

Competition, though friendly, is fierce and can be
deadly. At the high moment of the turn in the watercourse,
a canoe perhaps fifty feet long, which must be steadied and
turned without loss of a breath in time or speed, can be
sliced in two by the sharp prow of an oncoming com-
petitor.

On witnessing such an incident at a race meet on Washington's Makah Reserve, a *National Geographic* photographer expressed shock at such ferocious tactics.

A member of the host tribe replied with a grin, "Why
do you think we spend so much time polishing the edge of
our paddles?"

And with a shrilling war cry, he made a swift gesture of
decapitation.

Surrendering to the chant, it is easy to imagine Dan's
stories of the mystical times, remembered from his grandfather's telling, when the giant first-growth timber still stood
on these ravaged mountains—when man cut new wood
only for dwellings and canoes; deadwood or driftwood was
for burning.

The canoes were sheltered then, not in fragile wooden
sheds, but by the wings of fir trees a thousand, two thousand years old.

Seeming so softly feathered, such trees were strong enough to carry the mightiest burden of snow and turn the arrows of storm-driven rain.

The canoes were further protected by cedarbark mats, through which neither heat nor frost could pierce. For in spite of their great size—some eight or nine fathoms long—they were often sculptured to the thickness of a young girl's finger.

These were the racing and hunting canoes. Marvelously swift and graceful, they were fashioned after the creatures for which they were named—the falcon, master of air; the salmon, falcon of the sea, as swift in pursuit and similarly shaped—the head rounded for speed, the wide powerful body sleeking back to a narrow tail.

Such canoes rode easily above the waves. But for travel in the heavy seas beyond the sheltered inlet, others were fitted with a high prow, carved and notched like a human heart. The powerful sweep knifed through dangerous waters, hunting silently.

Dan describes the methods of those days, when canoes were shaped by filling the rough-hewn hull with water in which heated stones were placed. The resulting steam expanded the cedar to the desired shape.

He tells how sometimes the inside surface of the hull was burned, and cedar cross-sticks inserted to bend the heat-expanded wood.[2] Tough thongs of cedarbark rope would lash the rests for the paddlers. Knotholes were filled with tiny cedar twigs, pounded to firmness with plugs and wedges of the same scented wood. Then, with a mixture of seal oil and red clay, the carver would polish the whole length, patiently, caressingly, at the same time speaking to the canoe.

For to him it was, like all things, alive. Its strength and spirit had grown in the wood for a thousand years before emerging to bring food, prowess in the hunt, the wealth of friends, and the test of manhood.

"Even in my father's day," said Dan, "I can remember how he would talk to the canoe. He'd stroke and pat it and say, 'Be good. Be strong. Carry us safely on this voyage.'

"Of course," he continued, "these racin' canoes of today —what we still call the 'war canoes'—are lower in the water, lighter in weight, and they're finished with modern materials, even fiber glass, which would horrify the old carvers. They rub them with wax to get a high racin' polish. Even if a person just smooths his hands over a canoe that's gettin' ready to go in the water, the carver feels that little bit of body oil will cut down the speed."

Generations of the George family have been carvers and championship builders. Two of Dan's brothers were master builders, and Dan himself, after carving many smaller canoes, made his first war canoe in 1963.

It is a beautiful craft, nearly fifty feet long, with an overall thickness of one inch, and perhaps half an inch at its thinnest point—a fragile container for seventeen-hundred pounds of surging flesh. A wide curve that runs almost the full length of the hull gives the canoe its great speed.

"This curve," says Dan, "seems to carry us right over even the heaviest waves. I've been told by some of the crews that they never, never felt such lightness. You'll notice lots of canoes begin to sharpen about twelve feet from the prow, so when the goin' gets rough, they cut through the waves instead of riding them, so they ship a lot of water. I studied the shape of the salmon when I was makin' that canoe."

As the afterglow of the April evening fades, we can no longer follow the canoes . . . only the chant, which grows stronger as the return journey accelerates. Women, laden with blankets, come to the beach to stand facing the sea . . . waiting in their "motionless alertness" for the safe return of their men.

There is some special spirit in this April evening that enables me to voice my feeling that the inner power expressed through the canoe rituals has always seemed to me the symbol of survival of the Indian. Out there—in their element of ocean—our culture cannot touch them. Out there, we cannot strip away, as we have tried to do everywhere else, the essence of their Indian-ness—the beauty of their manhood.

As I tell my feeling, Bob's face turns grave, and his normally rich, rollicking voice is quiet.

"What you feel is true. My uncle, who trained me, told me, 'It is a very, very serious thing to put your canoe in the water. To enter in a race you must be willin' to give everythin', not just be a passenger.

" 'Our people judge a man in life by the way he takes part in the canoe. If you make a good paddler and a winner, perhaps you can be like that in life too, no matter what the odds are.' "

He looks toward the sea: "Out there, we open all our energies. Sometimes I think, 'Why does an Indian still want to do this? Who will remember it?' "

Then sadly, in his sense of inevitably disappearing custom: "Sure . . . sure, it's in my heart, and it's in my brother's heart. But who will remember it?"

Dan's smoky voice embraces the quiet.

"When we were talkin' once," he turned to me, "you

asked me what I felt my greatest achievement was. Now that my life . . . my time . . . is runnin' out, I know that of all the honors given to me, my greatest achievement came when I was thirty-five years old. It was gettin' late for me then to be a champion puller. And I decided that if I was goin' to get anywhere in my life . . . to really achieve somethin' . . . I'd better do it.

"So I took my canoe and started trainin'. Every day for weeks and months, ten miles up and down the inlet. And that summer I cleaned up every race on the West Coast.

"And that, to me, is still the greatest achievement of my life."

The laughter of four generations drifts from the canoe shed. Scented fires glow against the sea, and in the farther waters glow reflections of the celestial campfires of departed braves, now being lit one by one along the pathways of the sky.

The wing-breath of a late-hunting heron stirs my hair, and ten years of images flood my mind.

Dan in his Plainsman's feathers, playing Hollywood Indian. Dan as Old Lodgeskins, enduring without murmur the frightful prairie cold. Dan clowning with Art Carney, Bob Hope. Dan on the platforms of universities honoring him . . . in the schoolroom . . . at the banquet tables of self-seeking businessmen. Dan acclaimed in Washington. Dan in the concrete, skyless arroyos of New York . . . in the lonely luxury of vast hotels.

So many Dan Georges, in so many places.

Yet still so firmly of this place. The champion canoe puller, the winner.

Turning to him I ask, "Dan, do you remember something else we talked about in this same place ten years ago, when there was talk of developing the Reserve and the mud flats?"

"Yes. And I remember my tears."

"Has that changed? Would you ever leave now?"

The smoke of his voice turned to steel.

"No. Not never. This is the place of my blood. *I was born here. And I'm gonna die here.*"

Under the echo of his voice, the last chant dies. Women move from the firelit shadows to surround their men with warm blankets. A covey of great- and great-great-grandchildren lights at Dan's feet, follows him up the gentle rise to home.

He stands at the window of the old house, cradling a drowsy child in each arm. He looks out over the dark waters, deeper into the night.

NOTES

TWO: Triumph . . .

1. The full story of Chief Joseph's flight is told in Merrill Beal's moving book, *I Will Fight No More Forever* (Seattle: University of Washington Press, 1966).

SIX: The Real World

1. A Haida canoe preserved in the Smithsonian Institution in Washington, D.C., measures 59 feet. The beam, 8 feet; height of stem, 7 feet; height of stern, 5 feet 3 inches; height amidships, 3 feet 7 inches. The Haidas undoubtedly used much larger canoes, for the size of first-growth timber was enormous. The largest timber ever shipped was taken from the forest that covered what is now the main street of Vancouver. When cut and trimmed, it measured a flawless 101 feet.

SEVEN: The Marathon Years

1. Many people believe that the custom of scalping originated with the white bounty hunters. A Kwakiutl lady told me, "The French, English, and Dutch frontiersmen paid bounty hunters to scalp each other, and the Plains Indians learned from them. Here on the Coast we never scalped. In big battles sometimes the warriors would behead enemy chiefs and others, since we had no photographs or other ways of proving who had been killed in battle."

EIGHT: Changes

1. The Squamish are the closest neighboring tribe to the Tsla-a-wats, and the tribe from which Amy George came. The Shuswaps are an Interior group, living in the beautiful Shuswap Lake area of British Columbia.
2. *Two Articles* (Neewin Publishing Company, nd).
3. 1972 statistics. In some areas this rate has grown with increasing despair over unemployment and overcrowding.

NINE: Days Along the Shore

1. The Taylor referred to is the late Fred "Cyclone" Taylor of the Hockey Hall of Fame.

TWELVE: The Rebellion at Duck Lake

1. Auxiliary film crew used to shoot sequences away from the core action, which are then cut in to shorten production time.

2. The original Duck Lake Rebellion, known also as the Northwest Rebellion, took place in 1885 and was the occasion on which Louis Riel, celebrated Métis leader of the earlier Riel Rebellion, was captured.

3. The authentic story of the life of the Indian martyr Almighty Voice was told by his parents to Chief Buffalo Child Long Lance, the distinguished Indian writer and actor, and was published in *Maclean's Magazine* of January 1, 1924.

4. Author of *There Is My People Sleeping* (Sidney: Gray's Publishing Ltd., 1970).

5. Director of *Les Ordres*, winner of the Canadian Film Award for Best Picture of 1975.

6. Largest of a group of islands at the north end of Lake Huron, the total population of which is 10,893. Approximately one-third are Indian.

THIRTEEN: Voyageur

1. Poem written for Dan and Amy by Dorothy Davies. See-see-um is the Great Spirit of whom Dan writes in *My Heart Soars* (Saanichton, B.C.: Hancock House, 1974).

2. Although this ancient method is rarely used today, it was seen by the author as late as 1973, on a small, remote West Coast Reserve. The old canoe-maker recalled how his own great-uncle, in his ninetieth year, had instructed him to "burn" the canoe before the spring sun reached its morning heat. Just after sunrise on a May morning, the inside of a forty-foot canoe was doused with an exact amount of kerosene, to burn the wood to the expansion point. Quickly, as the flames died, cedar slivers no more than half an inch thick were inserted at the lip of the canoe. This stretched the craft a good two inches.